Here to Stay

Here to Stay

~

Uncovering South Asian American History

GEETIKA RUDRA

Rutgers University Press

New Brunswick, Camden, and Newark, New Jersey, and London

Library of Congress Cataloging-in-Publication Data

Names: Rudra, Geetika, author.
Title: Here to stay : uncovering South Asian American history / Geetika Rudra.
Description: New Brunswick : Rutgers University Press, [2022] |
Includes bibliographical references and index.
Identifiers: LCCN 2021028835 | ISBN 9780813584034 (hardback) |
ISBN 9780813584058 (epub) | ISBN 9780813584065 (pdf)
Subjects: LCSH: South Asian Americans—Social conditions. |
South Asian Americans—History. | South Asian Americans—Ethnic identity. |
United States—Ethnic relations.
Classification: LCC E184.S69 R83 2022 | DDC 305.800973—dc23
LC record available at https://lccn.loc.gov/2021028835

A British Cataloging-in-Publication record for this book is available
from the British Library.

References to internet websites (URLs) were accurate at the time of writing. Neither
the author nor Rutgers University Press is responsible for URLs that may have
expired or changed since the manuscript was prepared.

♾ The paper used in this publication meets the requirements of the American
National Standard for Information Sciences—Permanence of Paper for Printed
Library Materials, ANSI Z39.48-1992.

www.rutgersuniversitypress.org

Manufactured in the United States of America

To my mom, dad, and brother, Ritwik.
Thank you for everything.

Contents

Here to Stay

Introduction

This is the story about how I searched for myself in the history of our country, only to discover a secret American history that helps us understand what makes us American.

The United States is my home, but like anybody who has felt like an outsider in their own family, I've struggled with feeling like I belonged. Any American citizen who has been asked by their fellow Americans, "Excuse me, but where are you from?" will know what I am talking about.

I was born in Queens in the early 1990s. My parents had immigrated from India a couple of years before, in the late 1980s. We lived in a two-bedroom apartment off the J train subway line on 117th Street. My elementary school, Public School 56Q, was south on 114th Street. The park where I ran track, Victory Field, was down Myrtle Avenue, a short walk away. School was the center of my world. Every day, my mom held my hand as we made the walk to school. (I never walked unattended.) We walked on Jamaica Avenue, past an Italian pizza joint called Alfie's, an Asian grocery store, a Hispanic bakery, and a pet shop owned by a very old man who claimed to own the world's oldest fish. Overhead, the J train rumbled, connecting my little corner of the world to New York City.

Public School 56Q, also called the Harry Eichler School (schools in the New York City education system, with some exceptions, are given numbers, not names, so this school is an outlier), was an imposing brick and concrete building on the corner of 114th Street and 86th Avenue. Its main entrance was behind a tall, black, wrought-iron fence and atop a high set of stairs. Every morning, the children of my neighborhood, Black, Chinese, Indian, and Hispanic elementary school students in grades two to five, corralled through the front door to go up a flight of stairs that ended at a large gray entry hall that doubled as a gym and assembly room. There, we were greeted by our teachers, friendly white women (they were mostly women) who, like clockwork, took attendance and made morning announcements. This was the liveliest part of our day. For a solid thirty minutes we had time to see friends from other classes and talk about what children talked about: Harry Potter and our favorite boy bands. At 7:30 a.m. sharp, we all stopped whatever conversation we were having and stood to face the large American flag at the entry of the auditorium and recited the Pledge of Allegiance.

My favorite subject in school was social studies, which combined lessons in history, civics, and government. I think my love of social studies, and eventually history, started at home. My parents are your everyday Americans. My dad always talked about politics during dinner. My mom watched movies like *A Few Good Men*. They asked for my opinions on the latest news coming out of the Bush White House. Our discussions meandered around points and counterpoints, but they always ended on one theme: the United States of America was the best country in the world. It was the only country where someone could make something out of nothing. And, according to them, it was the only country that let people live freely. My parents left India and purposefully chose to make the United States their home because they believed no other country could compare. This filled me with a sense of deep pride. I gravitated toward reading all I could about my country. Every school year, I read my history textbooks cover to cover. Our school didn't have a library. Instead, a cart of books was parked outside our classroom once a week before it moved to the next classroom. I finished every book in that cart in a month. When I finished the third grade, the fourth and fifth grade teachers allowed me to borrow their textbooks to read over the summer.

The history textbooks I read took me further than the J train ever could. I devoured stories about the struggles and bravery of

George Washington, Thomas Jefferson, and Benjamin Franklin. In their search for a new world that could provide a better life than the old world, I saw my parents. I imagined trekking past the Appalachian Mountains immediately after the Louisiana Purchase, and taking the Oregon Trail to the Pacific. I read about the Civil War with a childlike amazement that slavery could ever have existed in the United States. I read about New York's Erie Canal and immigration and all the wars we won and how these events shaped New York and it made it the home I knew and loved and thought just how cool it was that I was an American.

Right before I started the fifth grade, my parents moved our family to a small community on the north shore of Long Island. This was their American dream. They bought a house in a neighborhood with a great school for my younger brother and me. Instead of walking to school, I now took the bus. The MTA did not connect Long Island to New York City, so instead, we paid thirteen dollars for a one-way ticket on the Long Island Railroad.

Moving to Long Island seemed great in many ways. We had a backyard with giant trees and a swing set. My new elementary school had a library that was larger than our Queens apartment. I took the challenge of reading the library's entire collection of books, which was the largest I'd ever seen, very seriously.

One evening after school, my mom took my brother and me to the supermarket. We were standing in line, talking about my day. My mom asked questions about my teachers and homework assignments, which I answered diligently. An older white man stood in front of us. I noticed he was wearing a World War II veterans cap, and recognized the insignia from a book I had read about air combat. He was just about to finish checking out when he turned to us and said, rather innocuously, "Are you all Indian? I was stationed in Burma in World War II. You all speak English so well."

I looked at the man and back at my mom. She tightly smiled, polite but not eager to extend the conversation. I remember feeling confused and blurted without really thinking, "Well, of course my English is good. I was born here. I'm American."

The man didn't say anything. I'm not sure if he heard me. In the car ride home, my mom tried to brush off what happened. "You are Indian American, Indian and American," she told me. "When people look at you, they might assume you are only Indian because of how you look. Don't worry about it; how people look at you is not in your control. Be proud of who you are."

Listening to my mom, my confusion solidified into concern. There was something about me that made me different from that man. There was something about myself that man could see that I couldn't, and that something didn't seem good. It made him think he and I were not the same. I was different. This was not good.

I started seeing all the differences between me and the other kids in school. They had iPods, grandparents who served, and parents who didn't have to worry about family back home. By the sixth grade, girls were dyeing and highlighting their hair with shades of blond that would not look good on me. They were all white. I was brown. Even my books were troubling. I was different from every person I read, let alone admired. Nobody in my American history books looked like me.

At the start of the seventh grade, my classmates and I were assigned to read *A History of US*, a series of American history books. I had never read anything from the series before. The series' title is a pun that was not lost on me. The history of your country is your history. The history of the United States was supposed to be my history. Except, it wasn't.

The other students in my class were able to pinpoint how their grandparents or great-grandparents had been affected by the events we read about. As far as I knew, my parents' generation were the first South Asians in this country. I was born in the United States and, by birthright, an American citizen, but I was not an American in the popular sense of the word. My origin story, and the origin story of people who looked like me, was not represented in the American history books I loved so much. I had no roots in the country that was supposed to be my home.

Home is supposed to be a place of comfort. Home is where you are seen. And yet as the daughter of immigrants who chose to make

America their home, I couldn't see myself. I was stuck in limbo between what I looked like and who I was. Instead of an identity that I could share with others, I had an identity that made me feel alienated. I did not belong. I was an other. My teenage imagination ran wild with angst. What would Thomas Jefferson, a founding father of my country and someone whose writing I revered, have thought of me if we had ever met in 1776. Would he have thought that I, a young brown woman, was his equal? Was I who he had in mind when he declared independence and wrote, "We hold these truths to be self-evident"?

Through my high school and college years, I always found myself on the periphery of race in the United States. In 2008, my junior year of high school, Barack Obama became our country's first Black president. In my liberal corner of Long Island, people called his presidency a sign that we were now in a "post-racial America." The color of your skin was supposed to no longer matter, truly. From my vantage point, however, very little changed.

I started to see my own alienation reflected in how racism thinly veiled the public's perception of President Obama. People I knew, people who tended to be white, openly questioned if he could actually be a president for all Americans. I couldn't recall his white predecessors receiving the same concern. I started to feel that there were some Americans who had a very specific view of who was American and who was not. For Americans whose skin color was white, other white Americans were unquestionably American. People of color had to undergo a more complicated evaluation.

In 2010, I was living in New York City and attending college. Public demonstrations to protest inequalities in class and race were becoming more and more frequent. Occupy Wall Street activists took over Zuccotti Park to protest growing income inequality. A few short years later, Black Lives Matter activists took to the streets to protest police officers shooting and killing innocent Black men and women while they were simply wearing hoodies, jogging, and living. People were angry. Police brutality, one of the many symptoms of systemic racism, wasn't new. But we were talking about it at a volume that hadn't been reached before. Instead of living in a post-racial world, we were all living in a racial, racist world. The deep fissures ignored in American society were quickly revealing themselves under the Obama presidency. Everyday life in the United States had not lived up to the mythology of America.

In the summer of 2013, I was a digital reporter in the ABC News newsroom covering the George Zimmerman trial. Zimmerman was a white, Hispanic man on trial for shooting and killing an unarmed Black teenager named Trayvon Martin in Florida. The trial became a lightning rod for conversations about race-based inequalities and injustices deeply embedded in the American government that persecuted Black and Hispanic minorities in the United States. Covering the trial felt important and impactful. But as a brown South Asian American, I wasn't sure of my place in the conversation.

For as long as I can remember, I was taught and shown to silently carry my differences until I reached a point of acceptance. By virtue of the color of my skin and where my parents were from, it didn't matter if I thought that I was American or considered myself an amateur American history buff. When people looked at me, they would assume I was always from somewhere else. This was my responsibility to bear. As a first-generation South Asian American, I had to earn the respect of mainstream (a coded word for white) America. This involved being obedient, unobtrusive and successful, or as it's called, a perfect model minority. I digested this responsibility, but the promise of an eventual acceptance tasted sour. What was it about this country that simultaneously promised to be a land for all people but treated its own citizens so differently because of something as arbitrary as the color of our skin?

The American history books I read during this time did little to answer my questions. The courses I took in college taught by the likes of Eric Foner and Casey Blake, some of the greatest American historians of our time, revealed that the history I was exposed to as a student and as a reader was incredibly biased and incomplete. The history I was taught was from a white American point of view, and it said more about who was in power than of the events that actually happened. America's original sin (as Jim Walls defined it in his book *America's Original Sin: Racism, White Privilege, and the Bridge to a New America*), racism, created a quagmire of conflict and contradictions that shape our divisions to this day. Although my history courses in college were far more illuminating than anything I learned in grade school, the spectrum of characters was still largely white. I resigned myself to a place of observation, leveraging my time as a reporter and a student of history to cover race in the United States wherever I could. It was my job to be on the outside, keenly aware of what was happening on the inside.

The year was 2014 and I was researching civil rights litigation in Columbia University's Butler Library for a reporting project. I stumbled across a paragraph that described a twentieth-century American court case on a website. This case changed everything for me. It was heard in a courthouse in Washington State. The year was 1913. The plaintiff was the United States. The defendant was someone named A. K. Mozumdar. I caught my breath. Mozumdar is a common name in Bengal, India, the same state where my father was born. I knew many people in Queens with the last name Mozumdar. But they were all new. As far as I knew, the history of people from India in the United States didn't begin until the 1960s at the earliest.

Here was evidence telling me otherwise and staring me right in the face. Even more interesting to me was that this court case was centered on Mozumdar's citizenship. I realized that since there was a South Asian man trying to become a citizen of the United States in 1913, there must be other South Asian characters in American history. I just had to find them.

I started by reading everything I could about the Mozumdar citizenship case. The case hinged on the Naturalization Act of 1790. This law prohibited nonwhite people from becoming American citizens. This discovery was astonishing. The law had been amended only once, to allow freed slaves and their descendants to become citizens, and was an active law until 1952. Learning this fact was shocking. I was realizing that the history I had been looking for my whole life, the history that I thought did not exist, actually did exist. And more disturbingly, the history was a story of people who looked like me being excluded from becoming American citizens.

In 2015, I had saved enough to leave New York by myself for the first time and set off on a research journey that spanned three years and took me to different corners of our country. I started in the Pacific North West where I tracked Mozumdar's early years in this country and the population of South Asian immigrants that worked the lumberyards in the 1900s. Next, I traveled to California where Mozumdar's story gave way for a group of South Asians to own successful businesses, start families, and even try to spark a revolution to free India from British colonial rule. I realized that these stories of South Asians in the United States were not only older than I thought but also larger.

As I discovered the stories of these brown "pick yourself up by your bootstraps" men and women, I also discovered an American unease with whether they could become Americans. The United States of the 1900s depended on immigrants just as it does today but had a very specific idea of who was an acceptable immigrant. They were white and able to assimilate in a way that after some time they would be indistinguishable from mainstream America. All this was codified by the Naturalization Act of 1790. "Whiteness" was defined as the most important qualification for prospective citizens in the United States. This was a literal, stark example of institutionalized racism in the modern United States. And this squarely impacted me. For a long time, I sat on the sidelines of the racial conversation, but now I had a part in it. It was time to reclaim whatever pieces of South Asian American history I could find.

I traveled to Washington, DC, to find out how a government built on the promise to be for everybody could so easily divide who could be and who could not be American. All the while, one hundred years after the events of my research, our country sped through the later years of the 2010s. Our country was divided over basic beliefs around who and what constituted the identity and soul of the United States.

The truth is that the people living in our country have always been more diverse than the people in our country's government, than the people depicted in our country's culture, and by far more diverse than the people included in our country's history. What this means is that the American promise of being a country for all, where all men, women, and children are created free, isn't really a promise but instead an experiment. It is our responsibility as citizens of this country to ensure this experiment is working. And that is my intent with this book.

I did not grow up seeing people who looked like me in the pages of my American history books because the people who wrote those books did not look like me. People who look like me, for too long in this country, couldn't fathom becoming historians or activists, politicians or businesspeople, when they couldn't even become American citizens. The result is that for a significant period of American history, South Asians (and Asians, Africans, Hispanics, and others from non-European parts of the world) were systematically denied citizenship based on the color of their skin. And this is almost entirely unknown to citizens of color in the United States today.

It is no wonder to me, then, that in the wake of national conversations about race, justice, and equality, often through the lens of the grave injustices and legacies of slavery that impact so many Americans today, many immigrants do not know how to participate in the conversation. We are implicitly told, by having our own history of suppression ignored, that this conversation is not ours to participate in. We don't have the same history. We are too new.

None of this can be further from the truth.

An American is someone who respects the past but is not burdened by it to step into the future. An American cares about creating a world that is just and fair for everybody. She believes that everybody has the right to live a life and raise a family free from harm or oppression. She believes that there is more that unites us than divides us. Everybody has come to this country either as an immigrant or the descendant of an immigrant. We come from all over the world. What makes us Americans is not the color of our skin but the shared belief that together we can create a world that is better than what we inherited. And America, for all of its faults, is designed to continuously improve.

This was a common theme in all of my research. Every person I encountered, either in the present day or in the pages of the past, strove for something greater than their current reality. This is what makes us American.

In this book, I tell the story of South Asian Americans and their fight for citizenship in the United States. I also tell the story of my research, and wherever possible, I dive into how I conducted my research with the hope that I can empower readers to make their own initiatives for research and discovery. The world of South Asian American studies has a lot of room to grow. I have a feeling I've only barely scratched the surface with this book. It will take the work of many more people to reclaim our complete history.

A country's history is not just a set of facts and dates. It is a portrayal of how the country sees itself. To truly feel accepted in America, I had to see myself in American history. And to change how America sees itself, it is my hope to share this story with as many people as I can.

New York
2021

1

Who Gets to Be American?

New York City, 2015

Columbia University on 116th Street in Manhattan is home to one of the largest research libraries in the world. Its collection is big. The weight of its millions of books and rare artifacts once threatened to sink the Ivy League university's campus into the depths of Manhattan island (probably to the glee of its downtown neighbor New York University). According to campus legend, the threat of too many books spawned the university's modern library system. Most books and materials that are part of the Columbia Library System now exist in facilities across the New York metro area. But a vast collection still exists on Columbia's campus, anchored by Butler Library.

Butler Library sits on a large stretch of 114th Street overlooking the Columbia campus. It's a neoclassical building with the names of dead, white men, pillars of Western and American culture, etched on its stone facade. The names include everyone from Plato and Aristotle to Herodotus (considered the father of history), and to Benjamin Franklin and Abraham Lincoln. Inside Butler are several stories of bookshelves. These shelves run uninterrupted along dark corridors that make up the building's inner core. There is literally nothing but stacks of books, and as such, students have taken to calling the innards of the building "the stacks."

I was sitting in the stacks but ignoring all the books around me. Instead, I was on Google. It had been a week since I discovered

Akhoy Kumar Mozumdar's petition for citizenship in a federal court in Washington State court in 1913. The initial shock of seeing a South Asian last name in the records of American government over one hundred years ago was worn away. It was the fall semester and studying for finals and searching for jobs after graduation had gotten in the way. Still, the curious idea that there were Indians living in the United States way earlier than the history books made its way to the back of my mind. That's how I found myself here, secluded from the rest of campus and surrounded by books that did not have anything I was looking for. Instead, I was on Google. Using the search browser, I looked up terms like "Mozumdar United States," "Early South Asian Americans," and "South Asian American history." I tried other iterations like "Hindus United States history," "Punjabis United States history," and "Bengalis United States history." I used broader queries like "Asian immigration" and "Immigrants from Asia United States."

I had access to millions of books through the Columbia library system. With Google, my searches crawled through over 35 trillion web pages in less than a second. And in the depths of the internet, I found websites that offered a story of American history I had never before heard.

There was much more to American history than I had been told. My search results revealed there were not many books on the subject, but there were a couple. None of these books were readily available and had to be preordered. I worked with a stacks librarian to track down copies of *Bengali Harlem* by Vivek Bald, *White by Law* by Ian Haney Lopez, and *South Asian Americans*, written in the '90s by Karen Leonard.

These books, and a couple of others I've included in an endnote of this book, were vital in my research. And I'll admit that I kept these in the tiny bedroom I rented on the top floor of a fifth-floor walk-up in Harlem, well past their due dates.

Apart from these books, the information I needed was all digital. A website maintained by a group of Mozumdar's followers contained not just a biography but also photos of Mozumdar in the United States at the turn of the twentieth century. An online collection of legal briefs contained the actual, digitized court documents from Mozumdar's case. Another online collection cataloged and made searchable local newspapers from the founding of the United States to the present day. I could search for Mozumdar's name and find newspaper articles about him during his lifetime. I discovered a treasure trove of primary source materials about South Asian Americans in the United States called the South Asian American Digital Archive. Here, I discovered that there was not one but what looked to be many Indians living in the United States at the same time as Mozumdar. Their photographs, diary entries, and immigration records were all online and accessible to anybody who knew where to look. My curiosity ran wild with the hundreds of stories of men and women who were part of the American tapestry but were now largely forgotten. For the last four years, I was a student of history and American studies at one of the best academic institutions in the world, and I had never been told this history existed.

What was especially egregious for me was that I had never been taught about the Naturalization Act of 1790. It was a website called Immigration History that brought to light that before 1952, only white immigrants to the United States could become American citizens. Reading this in the harsh blue light of my laptop screen, the last twenty-three years of my life seemed to come into sharp focus. I recalled every instance where someone, usually a white person, asked me, "Where are you from?"

They were people alive at a time when it was illegal for someone like me to become a citizen. Of course, they would assume today I was not an American. They grew up in a world where Americans were white. And although a law can change overnight, it takes much longer to change hearts and minds. The world I lived in was only forty years after the repeal of the racial restrictions set in 1790. Unbeknownst to me, I was surrounded by the legacy of a lie that Americans could only look a certain way when in reality we have always been diverse. Now that I knew, what could I do except try to reveal the truth to everybody else?

But first, I had to discover all I could about the history and legacy of immigration in the United States. There is no better place to be than New York City for learning about the history of immigration. During the great waves of nineteenth-century immigration, Ellis Island was the first stop for many immigrants arriving by boat to the United States, only to be replaced by John F. Kennedy International Airport years later.

These immigrants, although by today's standards were all almost universally white, sparked among the non-immigrant population of the United States questions on who could be an American and who could not. And at the heart of this debate was something more existential. Who was an American? To answer this question, I looked to a relatively unknown book that was recommended to me by a college professor written by Thomas Jefferson centuries ago, *Notes on the State of Virginia*. For most Americans, Jefferson's most famous piece of writing is probably the Declaration of Independence. But for many scholars, Jefferson's most influential writing, based on its influence on the trajectory and character of the United States, is *Notes*. Funnily enough, the story of how *Notes on the State of Virginia* came to be starts not in Jefferson's native colonial Virginia but in Philadelphia.

Philadelphia, 1779

François Barbé-Marbois had a question. Actually, the Frenchman, born in Metz in 1745, had twenty-two. Marbois had recently arrived in Pennsylvania colony to serve as secretary of the French legion to the thirteen colonies. In Philadelphia, Marbois found what he was looking for when he left his home country for the British colonies in the New World: a city that was full of Enlightenment promise without the yoke of history. Marbois was an early example, and certainly not the last, of an immigrant who marveled at the promise of America. There was little like it in Europe. Something about America allowed Marbois to enjoy a success in his new home—he was a tutor to French aristocratic children who would later go on to found modern charitable drives and marry the daughter of Pennsylvania's governor—that would have been much harder elsewhere. And like many immigrants after him, Marbois was to play a central role in the consciousness of what it meant to be an American.

In Marbois's time, Philadelphia was one of the fledgling United States' largest cities. The original plans for Philadelphia drafted by the city's founder, William Penn, in the first decade of the eighteenth century reveal an organized city divided into a grid of eight blocks by twenty-two blocks, bounded by two rivers: the Delaware to the east and the Schuylkill (Dutch for "hidden creek") to the west. (What was once considered to be the entire expanse of Philadelphia fits neatly between present-day South and Vine Streets.)

Philadelphia was the center of American cultural and intellectual life. Most importantly for Marbois, this thoroughly modern city on a hill was the center of American government.

Enticed by the image of the bootstrapping, honest, and hardworking American, who fought for freedom against an age-old adversary (an image perpetuated by Benjamin Franklin, one of the first real celebrities of French society), France agreed to help the American colonies in their war of independence from Great Britain. But aside from the romantic notions of what a fledgling America could be (fed into the French imagination, once again, by Franklin), the French actually knew little about this new people they agreed to aid.

In 1777, France became the first country to recognize the just-declared-independent United States. The French were motivated by two factors: an unrelenting historic rivalry with England and an enthusiasm for the ideals the French believed the American Revolution embodied. America had captured the French imagination as the land where a man could make it from rags to riches with reason and hard work. And yet, the French knew very little about life in the thirteen colonies. Secretary Marbois thought he could rectify this and gave a list of questions to the more influential members of the Continental Congress, the colony's first form of government. The questions ranged from queries about a colony's geography and resources, to the people who lived there, where they came from and what customs and beliefs they practiced. One of the members who received Marbois's questionnaire was thirty-seven-year-old Thomas Jefferson, the governor of Virginia.

The timing could not have been worse. The traitor Benedict Arnold had led British forces to capture Richmond, Virginia's capital. Jefferson and his government were forced to evacuate the city. However, it was when his newborn country's survival seemed most grim that Jefferson began a thorough inquiry into what exactly made America America. The result was *Notes on the State of Virginia*, a book that historians today consider to be one of the most significant American works published before 1785. In *Notes*, Jefferson provides an optimistic vision of a United States where Americans are farmers who own and work their own land, cultivating a work and civic ethic that would permeate through the strata of society and government. And yet, the society that Jefferson envisioned did not include African slaves and their descendants (or Native Americans and their descendants). Jefferson addresses slavery briefly, only to say that he believes their emancipation would be inevitable. The real question for Jefferson was what to do with newly freed slaves.

Jefferson could not envision a United States of America where both races coexisted. "Deep rooted prejudices entertained by the whites," Jefferson wrote, "ten thousands recollections, by the blacks, of the injuries they have sustained; new provocations; the real distinctions which nature has made; and many other circumstances, will divide us into parties, and produce convulsions which will probably never end but in the extermination of the one or the other race." It would be impossible for multiple races to live alongside in the United States. The solution? After emancipation, the United States would send the newly freed slaves to a colony (probably in Africa) that would receive the protection and resources of the parent country. In turn, the United States would promote white immigration to the United States in equal number to the slaves who would be forced to leave.

Indeed, it is out of Jefferson's prediction that the deportation of freed slaves to a colony outside the United States would create a vacuum in the country's labor supply that he became an ardent supporter of immigration to the United States. This need for population growth was a driving factor for independence when he drafted the Declaration of Independence in 1776.

England's attempt at sabotaging immigration efforts to the New World was cited in the declaration as cause for independence. In an often-overlooked passage of the declaration, Jefferson wrote of King George III, "He has endeavored to prevent the population of these States; for that purpose, obstructing the laws for naturalization of foreigners; refusing to pass others to encourage their migration; hither, and raising the conditions of Appropriations of lands." The survival and prosperity of our country, Jefferson knew, was contingent on population growth.

The first set of laws to govern the United States were the Articles of Confederation, an agreement among the thirteen states that created a system of government in which most powers were vested in the states, which were held together in a confederacy that acted together for situations like war. Under the Articles of Confederation, each state was allowed to create its own process of citizenship. The fourth article of the confederation read, "that the free inhabitants of each of these States, paupers, vagabonds, and fugitives, from justice, excepted, shall be entitled to all the privileges and immunities of free citizens in the several states; and the people of each State shall, in every other, enjoy all the privileges of trade and commerce." The language was confusing and led to different interpretations of the law by the thirteen states.

That the Articles of Confederation did not offer a uniform method for naturalization was one of the reasons James Madison believed that the articles had to be replaced. In 1788, he wrote, "The dissimilarity in the rules of naturalization has long been remarked as a fault in our system, and as laying a foundation of intricate and delicate questions. . . . The new constitution has accordingly, with great propriety, made provision against them, and all others proceeding from the defect of the Confederation on this head, by authorizing the general government to establish a uniform rule of naturalization throughout the United States."

Meanwhile, the U.S. population continued to grow. By 1790, the year the first census was conducted, we had reached a population of 3,929,214—just shy of 4 million people. But we still did not have a uniform system to naturalize immigrants into citizens. In his first message to Congress on January 8, 1790 (a practice every successive president would adopt and would later become the State of the Union), President George Washington urged the first Congress to create such a system. "Various considerations also render it expedient," Washington said, "that the terms on which foreigners may be admitted to the rights of citizens should be speedily ascertained by a uniform rule of naturalization."

This country's first laws on citizenship, immigration, and naturalization were not made in Washington, DC. In 1790, Washington, DC, was nothing more than a mosquito-infested swamp, hardly at the forefront of postcolonial American intellectual thought. This distinction was held by Philadelphia, a metropolis by the standards of the day. (Washington, DC, would later become home to American political life due to one of the many compromises made between the North and South.) The members of this country's first congress met in Congress Hall, a two-story building made of brick. Members of the House of Representatives met on the first floor, and members of the Senate met on the second floor. The central question that underpinned the discussion of citizenship and naturalization among the members of the first Congress was simple: Who could be an American?

Half of the American population immediately following the American Revolution were descendants of English immigrants. A quarter were descended of, or immigrants from, Ireland, Scotland, Wales, and Germany. The remaining quarter were slaves. (Most Americans were farmers, like Jefferson predicted, although occupations in cities were more varied.) Some of the first members of Congress were themselves immigrants, such as James Jackson of Georgia. Jackson was born in Devonshire, England and emigrated to Georgia in 1772 to study law. He would enjoy a successful political career as governor and was known to enjoy street fighting and duels (he killed at least one man in a particularly bloody brawl).

Despite having emigrated to the United States, Jackson was a nativist who believed in the strictest regulations for naturalization. Like other nativists of the first Congress, he was afraid immigration would jeopardize the carefully cultivated character of the fledgling republic.

John Page of Virginia, a slave owner, disagreed with Jackson. He advocated for immigration and believed in the promise that America offered to foreigners looking for better lives. "We shall be inconsistent with ourselves," he said, "if after boasting of having opened an asylum for the oppressed of all nations, and established a government which is the admiration of the world, we make the terms of admission to the full enjoyment of that asylum and government so hard as is now proposed. It is nothing to us whether Jews, or Roman Catholics, settle amongst us; whether subjects of kings or citizens; and neither their religious or political opinions can injure us, if we have good laws, well executed." Jackson countered that every incoming immigrant should be vetted by a grand jury of American citizens. Page would have none of it. "We must add an inquisition," he deadpanned. "Indeed, I fear, if we go on as is proposed now, in the infancy of our republic, we shall in time require a test of faith and politics of every person who shall come into these states." At the most basic level, there were questions within the first Congress as to whether naturalization should include a residency requirement, a civic test, or an interview.

It is important that we pause to examine the language that up until this point had been used to figure out the question of who should be naturalized. The drafters of the Articles of Confederation used "free citizens," "free inhabitants," and "the people," interchangeably. John Page differentiated foreigners along religious lines, referencing Jews and Roman Catholics, and not racial lines. Indeed, religion as a divisive factor among people was much more pertinent to contemporary affairs of that day than class or race. It is also important to note that although most other aspects of American law and government were modeled after the British example, this could not be done with naturalization. English law had no applicable precedent to deal with naturalization. In fact, although the need to establish citizenship for people living within the borders of a state was clear, countries throughout world history have had a fraught relationship with defining who can be a citizen and who cannot.

At the time founding fathers had to determine who could and who could not (by definition the concept of citizenship is exclusionary), the two prevalent principles that governed citizenship in European nations were jus sanguinis and just soli. Jus sanguinis, or "right of blood" designated a person's citizenship to where their parents were citizens. "Jus soli" or "right of soil" designated a person's citizenship to where they were born. Naturalization, the process by which someone could move to another country, renounce their citizenship, and become a citizen of their adopted country existed since Ancient Greece but had not been applied at the scale it would be implemented in the United States. As such, the founding fathers had very little to inform their determination on who and how one could naturalize. This problem was uniquely American. And in asking who could be a citizen, what the founders really asked was who could be an American.

Jackson and Page, along with the members of the first Congress passed An Act to Establish a Uniform Rule of Naturalization on March 26, 1790. It conferred the opportunity for naturalization to "any Alien being a free white person, who shall have reside within the limits and under the jurisdiction of the United States for the term of two years, may be admitted to become a citizen thereof on application to any common law Court of record in any one of the States wherein he shall have resided for the term of one year at least, and making proof to the satisfaction of such Court that he is of good character, and taking the oath or affirmation prescribed by law to support the Constitution of the United States, which Oath or Affirmation such Court shall administer, and the Clerk of such Court shall record such Application, and the proceedings thereon; and thereupon such person shall be considered as a Citizen of the United States." And so, in this act came the first legal restriction of citizenship across racial lines. The 1790 act would be amended in 1795 and again in 1802 to increase the residency requirement, and then replaced by the Naturalization Act of 1870 to include freed slaves and their descendants. But the law of limiting naturalization to "free white persons" would remain in effect until 1952 and be the primary factor in which American courts assessed an immigrant's eligibility for citizenship.

More than one hundred years after Jackson and Page debated who should be allowed to become American, Israel Zangwill stood outside the Comedy Theater in New York City and declared the grand American immigration experiment had worked. It was September 6, 1909, and the crowds had gathered for the American premier of Zangwill's play *The Melting Pot*. Zangwill's play told the story of David, a Russian émigré fleeing the pogrom and searching for a world in America where "ethnicity has melted away." Zangwill was a tall and thin man, who wore wiry glasses that perched on the tip of his nose, without the side parts that typically hold glasses affixed behind a person's ear. Zangwill's hair was matted. The critical reviews of Zangwill's play were tepid at best. His drama was too trite, the production too simplistic. *The Melting Pot*, for Zangwill, represented the ultimate representation of his life's work. Born in London to a prominent Jewish family, Zangwill had devoted his intellectual life to the question of what could be done with the world's politically and economically oppressed. Of course, Zangwill wasn't occupied about the whole world; rather, much of his thoughts focused on the lower rungs of European society. It was Zangwill's hope that the future of the society would be without race or ethnicity, which he saw as barriers to progress. Although he never immigrated to the United States, choosing to stay in London, Zangwill had pinned his hopes for a world without race or ethnicity on the United States. Zangwill saw the United States as a haven for immigrants and wanted to celebrate that only in America could people come to the United States from anywhere in Europe and, regardless of their religious or political beliefs, could create a new life for themselves. In fact, the phrase "the melting pot," used in American classrooms all across the country to explain the metaphor of assimilation for immigrants to the United States, was made popular by Zangwill.

Even though the critics panned his play, the public loved it. The *New York Times* called the premise "a fine idea" but dubbed the production "cheap and tawdry." Nevertheless, the play did hit a chord among theatergoers, as it ran for a successful 136 shows.

It was during this period of immigration, which historians dub the "third wave," that the term "the melting pot" entered our country's cultural zeitgeist. President Theodore Roosevelt attended the play's opening in Washington, DC, on October 5, 1909. "That's a great play, Mr. Zangwill, that's a great play," he said. Was Zangwill's America actually a country where ethnicity had melted away?

We must first examine the context in which this question has been asked throughout the history of our country. The question of Americanness has come up usually in correlation to moments in time historians have identified as waves of immigration. But first, a brief history of immigration to North America, pre-America.

It is generally agreed upon by historians that the first people to immigrate to what would later become the United States were migrants from the European and Asian landmass who had traveled over a land bridge that connected modern-day Russia to modern-day Alaska. This land bridge called Beringia allowed for a number of migrations to occur. Historians have generally concluded that the Beringia was flooded approximately 12,000 years ago, ending Eurasian migration to North America. It is unclear how many people crossed Beringia. Historians have differed on their estimates to be anywhere between 10 million and 100 million people. Their migration into what would later become Canada, the United States, and Mexico became what historians call the pre-Columbian settlement of these respective countries (before Christopher Columbus's arrival in 1492).

The first European wave of immigration to what would become the United States began during the colonial era, which historians generally agree lasted between 1600 and 1775. During these 175 years, immigrants were largely from England, with a few from Germany and the Netherlands. The first successful settlement was established in Jamestown, Virginia in 1607. This was followed by settlements along the east coast in which tens of thousands of immigrants, again mostly English, settled areas that became Massachusetts, Connecticut, Rhode Island, and New Hampshire. The peak of English immigration during this period occurred during 1629 and 1641 in which approximately 20,000 English settlers arrived.

Immigration began to decline in 1640 as conditions that led to civil war in England in 1642 began to worsen. The rate of immigration from England decreased to less than 1 percent, making it equal to the colonial death rate. Population growth from the 1640s through 1776 was attributed to a high birth rate and low death rate within the population descended from immigrants. New immigration did not contribute significantly to population increases.

The first census for the United States of America occurred in 1790. It almost didn't happen when a number of public figures protested the government counting population demographics as an attack on personal privacy. In 1790, the largest group of people to come to the United States were Africans who were forced into enslavement and then sold. The second largest group of immigrants to come to the United States were the English and then the Ulster Scots-Irish. Immigration between this time and 1830 was sparse. During this time, the United States perhaps had for the first and only time in American history a significant number of emigration leaving the United States. In this case, it was Loyalists sympathetic to the English who were leaving for Canada after the Revolution.

Immigration picked up in the 1830s. According to the available census records, immigration between 1831 and 1840 quadrupled to 599,000 people, compared to previous years. Most of these immigrants were from Britain, Ireland, and Germany who were attracted to the prospect of cheap land (the U.S. government was practically giving way large tracts of farmland in the newly settled frontier).

This stage of American history is particularly important for our story because it led to the first rise of nativism as a political and social movement. The sudden increase in the immigration rate to the United States sparked a concern among a group of people historians call the nativists, who feared that the sudden influx of Irish immigrants threatened the purity of America. In the eyes of the nativists, who themselves were the descendants of immigrants, immigrants from Ireland were not fit to participate in a republican democracy because of their lack of virtuous qualities and their Catholicism (it was feared they would be more loyal to the pope than the Constitution). Nativists dubbed themselves "Native Americans" and founded their own political party called the Know Nothing Party (members were urged to keep their organization secret by responding "I know nothing" to questions about their political affiliations).

Anti-immigrant sentiment grew more salient in the second half of the nineteenth century, when the rate of immigration to the United States increased to an astonishing 9 percent. Immigration from Ireland alone tripled to just under 2 million people between 1841 and 1850. The Irish was officially the largest immigrant group, with Germans ranking second, the British ranking third, and the French ranking fourth. According to census records from 1850, the U.S. population totaled to 23.1 million people of which 1.7 million were immigrants and 2.2 million were foreign born. During the same period, the percentage of Americans who were native born decreased from 98.5 percent in 1830 to 90 percent by 1850.

Historians consider the period between 1850 and 1930 as the height of immigration to the United States. Steam-powered ocean liners that offered cheap passage across the Atlantic, the Great Famine, and the political uprisings in Europe led to over 25 million European immigrants coming to the United States. The increased volume of immigration was matched by an increase in the diversity of who was immigrating. Although the Irish, Germans, and British still constituted the largest immigrant groups, immigrants also came from Italy, Greece, Hungary, Poland, and Russia. They were also religiously diverse. By some estimates, over 4 million Jews immigrated to the United States at this time.

Up until now, we have gone through the mainstream history of immigration to the United States. White immigrants crossed the Atlantic, arrived in the country through Ellis Island beneath the shadow of the Statue of Liberty, and then moved westward across the United States, settling farms and building towns and cities. But there was another group who traveled to our country from the opposite direction. They crossed the Pacific and arrived through Angel Island, nestled in a blue-green cove in San Francisco and welcomed by towering palms, and settled eastward. But could they become Americans in the same way their East Coast counterparts could? First, they had to satisfy one question: Were they white? Can they be considered white?

Millions of immigrants were in fact welcomed to the United States as they provided cheap labor and votes for progressive politicians. The naturalization laws remained largely unchanged. Although immigrants faced discrimination—for example, shops in cities like Boston and New York prefaced job advertisements with "No Irish"—there were no legal barriers to their naturalization. They had to be "a free white person . . . of good character."

2

Mozumdar Crosses the Pacific

San Francisco, 2015

Aboard a ferry on a cool, sunny morning, I watched an island slowly emerge from the San Francisco Bay fog. Planning a research trip out west was not easy. I knew my research had to take me to Washington State and California. From my apartment in New York City, these places felt more foreign to me than India. I was not sure how many times I could make research trips, as I had a day job and a night job. In my planning, I had to optimize for two things: I had to visit as many places as possible and I had to learn as much as I could from each place.

The first step of my plan was to find a home base. Seattle was a natural choice. The city was my connection to Mozumdar and being there could open doors for my research. Next, I had to plan visits to two research libraries that kept appearing in the citations of my online research: the Bancroft Library in Berkeley and the Department of Special Collections and University Archives at Stanford University.

Back in New York, I accessed each library's online catalog and made requests to view any document related to South Asian or South Asian American history. I received emails from librarians that they would notify me when the materials were ready. With nothing else to do but wait for the day I could visit the libraries, I made my first official research trip to Angel Island.

To get to Angel Island, I took a short flight from Seattle to San Francisco on a tiny regional plane that exacerbated my fear of flying. From SFO, I took an Uber to the Mission District, where a friend let me crash on her couch. After dropping off my bags and picking up a burrito at the Mission's famed Taquería El Farolito (if I was going to travel this far for research, I was also going to enjoy the local food), I took another Uber to Fisherman's Wharf, a neighborhood on the northern tip of San Francisco's waterfront. As its name suggests, the neighborhood began to develop in the nineteenth century when Italian immigrants arrived and started businesses catching and selling fish to miners passing through San Francisco during the gold rush. Today, Fisherman's Wharf is a popular tourist neighborhood. It's located right on San Francisco Bay with views of the Golden Gate Bridge and direct ferry access to Alcatraz. Nestled between the seafood restaurants, souvenir shops, and parking lots full of tour buses is Pier 41. It was from Pier 41 that I purchased a seat for the next day's ferry to Angel Island.

When the ferry reached the shores of Angel Island, I walked onto the dock with a handful of other passengers. Most folks seemed to be going camping, as much of the island was declared a state park. They headed up the dirt trails, carrying their sleeping bags and backcountry gear on their backs, and I watched them until they disappeared into the trees. With the beach to my back and the island's forests and hillscape in front of me, I followed a paved road that was wide enough for golf carts. Even though internet here was choppy, I had the foresight of downloading a map on my phone. Using my downloaded map, I followed the paved road as it wrapped around the circumference of the island. As I walked deeper into the island, I saw fewer and fewer people until it was so quiet that I could hear the waves crash against the shoreline. The beach must have been close by the whole time. The paved path started to snake back to where I started, and my map guided me on a dirt path in the direction of a cove. I walked for a minute on the path until I saw it.

Among a group of trees and perched on the top of a cove were a colony of large, white buildings that a century ago served as an immigration station and detention center for immigrants from Asia. As I walked closer to the building, the dirt path became paved again and I noticed small stone monuments bordering the path. The stones were engraved with the names of immigrants who had come through here, with the names of their descendants who erected the stones in their honor. The stones were etched in Chinese, Japanese, and Korean. I thought of these men and women. These were the people whom history had forgotten, but their families in the United States never forgot. I thought of the rest of the men and women who were still unnamed.

I entered the main building on the station grounds and saw a plaque commemorating the sisterhood between Angel Island and Ellis Island, two immigration stations at opposite ends of the country. The plaque hung in a hallway that led to a series of rooms. These were painted a dull yellow color that, over one century later, remained untouched to preserve the writings the mostly immigrant men who were processed here etched into the walls. Processing at Angel Island could take up to ninety days, and for many unfortunate people, it took two years. In this time, immigrants had to wait in the adjacent detention centers. Rooms were tiny, beds were hard, and sending word to family back home was impossible.

This prolonged detention of immigrants is where Angel Island diverges from its East Coast sister's treatment of immigrant (although Ellis Island certainly had its trials). The writings on the wall around me, scrawled laments of people who were homesick and uncertain of the future, served as a detail that reminded me of the distinct tribulations that marked the beginning of Asian American life in America. I thought of the endless ships that came into this cove and the people in those ships who had no idea of the hardships they would face. I thought of their families back home, likely worried when they hadn't heard confirmation of their loved ones' arrival. And I thought specifically of the people who looked like me and walked these walls one hundred years ago, stuck between two worlds. To understand them and the convergence of their arrival to Angel Island in the 1900s and the context they would inherit from Asian immigrants in the nineteenth century, I needed to go back in time and much further than anticipated.

Calcutta, Nineteenth Century

In 1864, 400 million people lived in the British Empire. They covered 10 million square miles of land, just shy of half the total amount of earth's inhabitable land. Among its possessions, the British Empire claimed Antigua, the Bahama Islands, Barbados, Barbuda, the Bay Islands, the Bermuda Islands, British Guiana, British Honduras, Canada East, Canada West, Cape Breton Island, Cape Colony, Dominica, England, the Falkland Islands, Gambia, the Gold Coast, Gibraltar, Great Cayman, Grenada, Heligoland (right off the German coast in the North Sea), India (including modern-day Pakistan and Bangladesh), the Ionian Islands, Ireland, the Malta and Gozo Islands, Mauritius, Montserrat, New Brunswick, Newfoundland, the Northern Territory of North America, Novia Scotia, Prince Edward Island, Scotland, Seychelle, Sierra Leone, Saint Christopher Island, Saint Lucia, Saint Vincent, the Virgin Islands, Tobago, Trinidad, and Wales.

At the center of this empire, second only to London in population and esteem, was Calcutta. Calcutta was built to sprawl along the river Hooghly, which spilled out of the Indian east coast and into the Bay of Bengal. Along the banks of the Hooghly were white administrative buildings built in neoclassical and Gothic styles that were the fashion of urban planning in cities thousands of miles to the west. These buildings had tall and wiry spires that stabbed into the Indian sky like needlepoint and were painted a stark, clean white that fought off the layer of dust and dirt that seemed to leave everything a tinted sepia. Offices surrounded by sprawling green lawns on which white men dressed in white played orderly games of cricket stood side by side with huts that were thatched with the branches of indigenous palm trees. Ships with long, wooden masts that had collected thousands of nautical miles circumnavigating the globe were docked along the Hooghly, alongside small wooden canoes used to ferry international cargo to shore. There were buildings for men in government and buildings for men in religion. Here was the capital of British India and the crown jewel of the British Empire.

Calcutta in 1864 was a city of contradictions. It was the birthplace of Rudyard Kipling who described his home as "poverty and pride—side by side." It was the home of Nobel Laureate poet Rabindranath Tagore who wrote, "Something undreamt of was lurking everywhere, and every day the uppermost question was: where, oh where I would come across it?" Calcutta had been divided into two sections: white town and black town. In white town lived the British colonists and administrators, who built wide avenues and grand white mansions and government buildings that recalled the neoclassical architecture of European cities. In black town lived the local Indians, largely poor servants and workers who lived in shanties and huts. Straddling these two worlds were upper-caste Hindus, well-to-do families who comprised the city's political, cultural, and economic elite. Their wealth had increased after creating early alliances with the British but found themselves questioning the institutions and belief systems that had governed their lives before and during British rule.

It is this period of Calcutta's history that historians call the Bengali Renaissance. Historians agree that the founder of the Bengali Renaissance was Raja Ram Mohan Roy, who is credited with introducing the word "Hinduism" into the English language. Challenging religious preconceptions was just as important to Roy as questioning Calcutta's political norms. As he studied to be a pandit (a Hindu priest), Roy worked alongside Christian missionaries who had been brought to Calcutta by the British East India Company. Influenced by their monotheism, as well as his study of the Upanishads, texts that teach Hindu spirituality, Roy rejected regional interpretations of Hinduism that relied on ritual and social practices he thought had less to do with spirituality and more to do with social custom. It was this shift in Hindu thought that fueled Calcutta's intellectual reawakening, ultimately giving way to India's movement toward secularism and colonial independence. And it was in this year, at the height of the Bengali Renaissance, that Akhoy Kumar Mozumdar was born.

Mozumdar was born to a Hindu family that, he would later tell rapt audiences in America, was of a high caste. Calcutta's society was striated along the lines delineated by the varnas, classifications of society based on ideal occupations: the priests and scholars, the rulers and warriors, the merchants and businessmen, and the laborers and servicemen. It is possible that Mozumdar's family lived comfortably. Indeed, Mozumdar's father was an attorney, granting him access to wealth that would have been above average compared to the rest of the city. Mozumdar was the youngest of nine siblings. He had eight older brothers and one sister. His sister was his father's favorite and inherited the family's jewels. Mozumdar was sickly. He had bad eyesight, weak digestion, and was smaller than other children his age. Like other families of their stature, the Mozumdar family had servants. But Mozumdar's mother cooked his meals personally and cared for him with extra attention that was not given to her other children. Mozumdar would reflect later in his life on the special bond he believed they had shared.

Mozumdar came of age during what historians dub the Bengali Renaissance. Similar to the European Renaissance that had occurred almost four centuries earlier, the Bengali Renaissance saw an increase of intellectual fervor take hold of the city. Intellectuals questioned institutionalized social structures such as the caste system, patriarchy, and even colonialism. A particular amount of attention was placed on religious thought. Occurring at the same time as the Bengali Renaissance was the Brahmo Samaj movement, which counted many of the same intellectuals among its members. The Brahmo Samaj movement advocated for what its members called a Universal Religion, which sought to disconnect the fundamental tenets of Hinduism from the ritual and practices that had come to create the impression that Hinduism was a polytheistic faith with hundreds of regional interpretations.

It is unclear what Mozumdar's religious upbringing entailed, but he claims to have turned to religion when his mother passed away when he was sixteen years old in 1880. The events that followed the death of his mother are unclear. But according to accounts by Mozumdar's American disciples, Mozumdar was ultimately kicked out of his home by his father after an argument. Mozumdar's travels in this period of his life were varied, he told his disciples. He traveled to Jerusalem to study Christianity (Mozumdar's trip cannot be verified, but there does exist to this day a lodge in Jerusalem that was founded by Indians in 1200 traveling to the Middle East looking for a place to rest. The lodge would be used in World War II by the Indian Fourth Infantry division, fighting under the British Union Jack) and the Himalayas to study with ascetics. Mozumdar would also later claim to have traveled to Hawaii where he studied local spiritualism. Indeed, many of Mozumdar's stories he later told his disciples in America created a narrative of Mozumdar as a traveling seeker of spiritual truths. This was quite unlike what Mozumdar would more accurately become once in the United States—an entrepreneurial, self-proclaimed guru (the Deepak Chopra of his time), who would require citizenship to own land in California.

San Francisco, Nineteenth Century

Some historians argue that immigration to the West Coast predates immigration to the East Coast. (The arrival of Filipino workers in the fifteenth century, brought by the Spanish, is an example of this early immigration.) Herein lies the difference between West Coast and East Coast immigration: race. Immigrants from Europe arriving on America's East Coast were seen as the potential to affirm and augment what was thought of as the American citizen. They were for the most part white and could become white in the American sense. Immigrants from Asia arriving on America's West Coast were seen as a threat. They were not white and were perceived to be so unlike Americans in their way of life that they threatened to contaminate American society.

The first major wave of Asian immigration to the continental United States occurred in the middle of the 1800s when 25,000

Chinese immigrants arrived in California to discover *Gam Saan*, or "Gold Mountain," at the height of the California gold rush. The Chinese who came were mostly male and worked as laborers in San Francisco. The Chinese were immediately excluded from American society and relegated to impoverished ghettos that Americans would come to call Chinatowns, areas of scourge and blight in America's cities. In 1869, the *New York Times* described the Chinese immigrant population as "a population befouled with all the social vices, with no knowledge or appreciation of free institutions or constitutional liberty, with heathenish souls and heathenish propensities, whose character, and habits, and modes of thought are firmly fixed by the consolidating influence of ages upon ages."

Walter Lindley, Los Angeles' appointed health officer, summed this up in 1879 in one his first health assessments of the city. Chinatown, he wrote, was "a rotten spot." The arrival of the Chinese on the West Coast marked a period of fear that lasted through the remainder of the nineteenth century of the "yellow peril." The Chinese were incorrigible and unable to assimilate. How they looked, the language they spoke, and their customs and beliefs were all seemingly antithetical to American society.

Much of the opposition against immigrants from Asia was intellectualized to draw examples from the immigrants' culture or history. In reality, the opposition was described in blatantly racist tones, drawing on the immigrants' physical look and characteristics. As the historian Alan Kraut explains, immigrants were "repelled because their very appearance suggested to their hosts' gazes a physical inferiority or vulnerability that the native born feared might be contagious. . . . The Chinese, especially produced such visceral reaction in native-born Caucasian Americans." The distinction people made during this time period was clear: the Chinese were not white. Blocked from citizenship, they could never be American. Even their children, regardless of how long they lived in the United States, would always be nothing more than foreign.

By 1880, there were 105,465 Chinese and 145 Japanese living in the United States, concentrated mainly in California, according to that year's census. Since immigration from Asia was coming from China, this part of the world was the first to be targeted by anti-immigration laws. The Chinese Exclusion Act of 1882 was the first law to prohibit immigration based on a person's race or origin. The prohibition of Chinese immigration put a severe stress on American businesses that had been dependent on Chinese immigration for cheap labor. This demand was filled by immigrants coming to the United States from Japan. By 1900, there were 24,326 Japanese living in the United States. The population had grown, but nonetheless, they were not white, could not be citizens, and so could not be American.

The U.S. government's policies on Asian immigration at this time were largely driven by geopolitical understanding of these regions. Much of nineteenth-century Asia was controlled by empires. The Japanese Empire controlled modern-day Japanese islands and the Korean Peninsula. The Dutch controlled the East Indies: Borneo, Sumatra, Java, and the surrounding islands. China controlled land bounded by the Himalayas in the west, the Pacific Ocean in the east, and Outer Mongolia to the north. Bordering China to the south was the French colony of Indochina, modern-day Vietnam.

The remainder of the subcontinent, land that stretched from the Himalayan mountains to the Indian Ocean, belonged to the British Empire—the strongest colonial presence in Asia. What later become modern-day India, Pakistan, and Bangladesh was then called the British Raj, the crown jewel of Britain's colonial ambition. The United States had scant relations with the British Raj, as any diplomatic needs were conducted through the main channels in London. And yet India, as the region was colloquially called, played a role in how Americans imagined the East. In 1893, Narendranath Dutta, a Hindu monk dressed in orange robes and a yellow turban who assumed the name Swami Vivekananda, introduced Hinduism and yoga to the Western world at the Parliament of World's Religions in 1893 in Chicago. He was joined by other religious leaders of India, all of whom were invited to speak at the Art Institute of Chicago by the American lawyer

Charles Carroll Bonney. There was Hdarampala, a Buddhist and secretary of the Maha Bodhi Society of India, Virchand R. Gandhi, secretary of the Jain Association of India, and Hanoenara Nath Chakravati, a theosophist from India. "It was an inspiring spectacle," a reporter for the *Indiana State Sentinel* wrote on September 13, 1894, "when the principal party of those who were to make addresses of the day, all attired in their priestly robes, and wearing the insignia of their office marched in peace and fellowship to the platform, while the audience rose and cheered at the sight."

India had also captured the imagination of America's literary elite. Mark Twain traveled extensively through Britain's colonial possessions in 1895 and wrote in 1897 in his travel memoir *Following the Equator* that India was the only place that continued to captivate him after he left and the only place he longed to return. The classical Hindu religious text the Bhagavad Gita informed the thought and writing of American writers Henry David Thoreau and Ralph Waldo Emerson. But it was perhaps the English writer Rudyard Kipling, whose 1895 children's book *The Jungle Book* told the story of an orphan boy raised by animals in the jungles of India, who can be credited with bringing India to the mainstream American imagination. An India that was a fantastical and spiritual escape for writers, thinkers, and intellects dominated the American perception of the country in a way that Chinese or Japanese culture never did. Immigration from India had in no way reached the scale of immigration from China or Japan. When Akhoy Kumar Mozumdar arrived in the United States in 1905, he would have been a minority among minorities.

When people like Mozumdar arrived in the United States, they were not classified by their country of origin, like the Chinese or Japanese. They were not called Indians or British subjects. They were called "Hindoos" by Americans. That immigrants from the South Asian subcontinent were all labeled a misspelling of Hindu, and were often not actually Hindu, demonstrates a lack of understanding of Americans of who these people actually were. Were they mystical spiritual leaders who could have shared the stage with Swami Vivekananda in Chicago? Or were they high-caste Brahmins keeping the secrets of ancient texts like those in the imaginations of Thoreau and Emerson?

San Francisco, 2015

I spent much of my time walking around the grounds of the Angel Island detention centers. Despite the bleak history, it was beautiful. Dark gray cliffs rose from the clear blue Pacific water and gave way to lush trees and rolling green hills. Seeing past the cove became harder as the daytime fog rolled in. It was the island's isolation and seclusion that must have made it the ideal location for an immigration station. Compared with Ellis Island, where immigrants were greeted with the Statue of Liberty, Angel Island was all too quick to hide its immigrants and keep them removed from the mainland.

To leave the complex, I had to make my way back into the main immigration station. I made sure to do another round through all the rooms to take photographs and make sure my notes captured everything. Even though I knew South Asian immigrants had come through Angel Island from my Google searching, I couldn't find any evidence of them in the buildings. I entered a small room that I had missed before. This room contained a computer that I would have ignored if not for a sign that said with that computer visitors could access for free Ancestry.com. It never would have occurred to me to look for research on Ancestry.com. But I sat on a small stool someone had left for visitors and typed in "Angel Island." An incredibly long list of people appeared, each with a first name, last name, and year. These were people processed through Angel Island. I scrolled through the list. Some of the names were South Asian. I had an idea. In the same search bar, I typed Mozumdar's name. Nothing appeared. I tried again but this time making a more general search across all of Ancestry.com's premium database. A result appeared. Clicking on the link opened a window that was the scanned image of a handwritten naturalization document filed by either Mozumdar or someone on his behalf.

Excited, I zoomed into the image. I couldn't believe what I was seeing. In front of me was not only what might have been Mozumdar's signature but also the name of the ship that took him to the United States, the dates of his journey, and even the American port city where he landed. My excitement quickly turned into disappointment. I knew on arrival to Angel Island that in many ways my research trip would be difficult because over one century separated between me and my people of interest. I discovered a new obstacle. I was in the wrong place.

Seattle, 1905

The white ocean liner RMS *Empress of China* glided into Washington State's Puget Sound sailing under the British flag. The ship was part of a fleet that included two other ships: *Empress of India* and *Empress of Japan*. The three ships traversed the Pacific Ocean, delivering mail between England, Canada, and Hong Kong, connecting the west coast of North America to eastern Asia. *Empress of China* was painted a bright white and almost 500 feet long. It had two smokestacks and three towering masts. The ship could carry up to 600 passengers. On this particular voyage, the RMS *Empress of China* was carrying passengers who had left Tokyo, Japan on January 1, 1905 to come to Seattle.

Seattle in 1905 was a small town that was quickly bearing the signs of a fledgling city that would serve as a major transit point connecting the United States to Asia. The city's economic growth was fueled by the timber industry. Forests, thousands of years old, covered much of the land that would later be incorporated into what we know as Seattle and Tacoma today. It helped that San Francisco, 800 miles to the south, kept burning down. Timber from Seattle built San Francisco after fire, including the Great Fire of 1906, destroyed the city several times. The money from timber was followed by growth in the railroad industry, which connected Seattle to coal mines and the rest of western United States. As a result, Seattle became a major stop for people traveling across the Pacific Northwest in search of fortune during the gold rush, and service industries emerged to cater to them. In search of such jobs, Americans and European immigrants came to Seattle from the eastern United States. Seattle also had an influx of immigrants from the west—Asia.

Seattle's immigrant population was much more ethnically diverse than American cities on the East Coast. Immigrants from China arrived in Seattle and found work building its rail lines. They were joined by immigrants from Japan and the Philippines. By 1905, these communities had lived in the area for almost fifty years. Seattle did not have an immigration station to process people arriving on their shores, and many immigrants came on commercial ships carrying more goods than passengers from Hawaii and the South Pacific. It is unclear what the exact population of immigrants from the British Raj were living in Seattle at the time. Indeed, newspapers from the time do report that a number of "Hindoos" were living in Oregon and Washington State, working largely at lumber mills. When the RMS *Empress of China* docked in Seattle on January 22, 1905, after a three-week voyage from Tokyo, Mozumdar disembarked the vessel, determined to follow a destiny that was far different from the "Hindoos" who labored over lumber.

3

The American Dream

John F. Kennedy International Airport, 2015

My flight to Seattle from New York City was overbooked and late. I was going to the West Coast for a three-month reporting trip for this book. As an anxious flyer, I was nervous. As a first-time book researcher, I was also apprehensive. I worried about how futile my attempt at finding anything about Mozumdar or what he did over a hundred years ago would be. Planning this trip was hard. I kept checking my phone to see if any of the librarians from Berkeley or Stanford got back to me. They hadn't. I was about to board a flight to a city where I had no idea what to do once I landed. Seattle felt like the right city to live during my reporting trip because it was where Mozumdar lived, but I had nothing planned. Perhaps it would be best to take a flight after a couple of days in the city down to San Francisco. The thought of another flight so soon put my fear of airplane crashes into overdrive. I took to people-watching JFK's departure gate to distract myself.

My parents immigrated to New York in the 1980s. According to the U.S. Census Bureau, my parents were two of 5.7 million people who immigrated to the United States that decade from all over the world. Like many others, they navigated a complex set of immigration laws, saved money for the trip, and braced for the emotional uncertainty that came with upending their roots for a country where they knew no one. They each flew into JFK and settled in Queens. They met when they were the only Indians living on their block in Queens. They got married and had me.

I was born in Queens, and in the 1990s Queens had one of the largest concentrations of Asian and South Asian immigrants in the New York area. It was the norm in public schools to be an immigrant or a child of immigrants. Every so often, a friend would have a lucky day off to attend their parents' naturalization ceremony (or, by extension, their own). I saw our neighborhood, in a span of a few short years, transition from being mostly white to mostly brown. Our white neighbors were moving to the suburbs of Long Island, and it was the aspiration of every Indian family we know, including our own, to follow. One by one, my parents' friends accomplished the dream: buying a home on Long Island (or New Jersey) where there were fewer immigrants and better schools. Finally, one day, it was our turn.

We moved to a suburb of Long Island just thirty minutes away from the city by the Long Island Rail Road in 2002. Roslyn was mostly white, Jewish, and upper class. There were some Indian families in our town, and they were quite different. These families were older and more established. My parents told me they were "professionals." Many of these uncles and aunts (as I was told to call them) were doctors. They had done the same my parents had done—leave India, land in JFK, live in Queens, and then move to Long Island. But their American dream was accomplished twenty years earlier as part of a wave of immigration from Asia and South Asia that addressed the need for more doctors and engineers in the United States. These families had more time to accrue wealth in the United States; their children were more assimilated. Looking at them made me envision what my own parents would be like after twenty more years of living in the United States.

As my plane to Seattle took off and I peered over the wings of the plane from my window seat to the New York metro area 30,000 feet below, it was hard to imagine the millions of immigration stories that packed such a tiny swatch of geography. It was even harder to imagine these stories outside of New York or even stories that predated the 1960s. So much of my knowledge of history was centered on the East Coast. I had so much to learn, though I never would have imagined expanding my knowledge of American history in this way. I always thought it was far more likely that I would visit Seattle on a tribute trip to Nirvana, whom I listened to so much growing up, than on a trip to learn more about South Asian American immigration history.

From what I knew at the time, based largely on what friends told me, Seattle was a mostly white city with some pockets of Asian and South Asian immigrants who worked in its tech industry. I had one cousin who, with her husband, both worked as software engineers and were sponsored by Amazon on H-1B visas. The flight was uneventful, thankfully, aside from the epic view of Mount Rainier we could see just before landing. My first impression after getting picked up by a cab driver and driving down Interstate 5, a stretch of highway that runs through Seattle, was just how wide, open, and green the spaces were. I was staying in Seattle's Capitol Hill neighborhood, and I spent my first few days walking around. At first, the city did feel quite different from home, demographically and culturally. The people I walked by on the streets were less diverse than my neighbors in New York. Even their interests were different. (Imagine a lot of craft beer, Patagonia, and weekend trips to the outdoors.) However, there were challenges to my first impression. The first was Seattle's Asian Art Museum, one of the only institutions in the United States dedicated to only Asian art. The second was the Quest Book Shop, a new age bookstore on Broadway (the name of the street made me scoff when I walked by). When I walked inside, I saw a section called Christian Yoga. In that section, on a shelf facing the store's entryway, was a bright blue book with an image of a cross and a female figure meditating titled *The Life and the Way* by A. K. Mozumdar. The book was published in 1911, six years after Mozumdar arrived in the United States.

Despite having left home, Mozumdar must have kept some contact with his family in Calcutta. According to accounts written by his followers, when Mozumdar arrived in Seattle, he received an allowance of nine dollars a month from his family. He was taken in by a Swedish family, Jennie and Charles Clark, living in Seattle's Swedish quarter (the present-day neighborhood of Ballard). In Mozumdar the Clarks found a young man who weighed only 110 pounds (according to a newspaper account written years later) and could not speak English well. The earliest known photograph of him shows a young man dressed in long robes with a sash around his waist, like a priest. He stands with hand at his hip, facing the camera but staring upward, as if looking at something behind but above the viewer. His nose is long and sharp, his hair is thick and parted to the side, and his moustache is groomed and curled at the ends. The photograph was taken in a studio, and unlike the photographs of Mozumdar that were taken later in his life and in more casual settings, has the studied sense of someone trying to create an image of how they want to be seen to the rest of the world.

Together, Jennie and Charles Clark and Mozumdar were members of the Theosophical Society. The Theosophical Society was a national organization founded in 1875 in New York City (today, it has over sixty chapters and its international headquarters is in India) by Helena Petrovna Blavatsky, the first Russian woman to become a naturalized American citizen, and Henry Steel Olcott, an American colonel and a veteran of the American Civil War who was part of the commission to investigate President Abraham Lincoln's assassination. The society sought to discover the truths that would let them understand the universe and the nature and the reason of human existence. Blavatsky and Olcott traveled to India in 1878 to establish their international headquarters in Adyar, India. Theosophy, according to Blavatsky and Olcott, was the study of the spiritual knowledge known by mystics, sages, and gurus. By 1903, the Theosophical Society had recognized chapters in every major American city that were allowed to operate by charter at the international headquarters' behest. Organizations like the Theosophical Society were part of a growing religious trend in the United States that Mozumdar benefited from on his arrival to the United States.

At the society, Mozumdar found a group of people who welcomed discussions and teachings about Eastern and Western spiritualism, and the Clarks and their members welcomed him back, according to his follower Emma Suydam. She would write later in a memoir that Mozumdar's first speeches were given in an abandoned store where he stood atop an orange crate.

In 1906, Mozumdar moved to Spokane, Washington. Spokane was home to the First Society of Christian Yoga, and Mozumdar would become a teacher of "Christian yoga," and later considered a founder of the organization. He had an address listed in the Spokane white pages as Apartment 12, S 320 Browne. Mozumdar spoke at the homes of First Society members and traveled from town to town in the Pacific Northwest giving lectures. The *East Oregonian* (which still publishes today) ran an article in 1908 that described one such evening when Mozumdar held a talk at the home of a couple with the last name Terpening in Pendleton, Oregon.

"A large attendance of interested listeners greeted Professor Akhoy Kumar Mozumdar, the well known Hindu philosopher and teacher, at the residence of Mr. and Mrs. C.S. Terpening last evening. He gave a delightful exposition of the Yoga philosophy and teachings and will organize a class in the Yoga healing to meet at the Terpening residence. A large number of Pendleton people have during the past few years, and Professor Mozumdar finds many well advanced in this line. He will remain in the city for several weeks perhaps."

There's a lot that an amateur history buff can glean from this paragraph. The reporter gave Mozumdar the title of professor. Although there are claims made by his followers that Mozumdar studied and taught in an American university (Berkeley and Columbia have both been mentioned), none could be confirmed with a primary source from a university. Whether the reporter called Mozumdar a professor by Mozumdar's instruction or by his own inference, the title was never corrected.

The article also references yoga in a way that suggested the reporter's audience was already well aware of yoga. Pendleton, Oregon in 1900 had a population that was a little less than 4,500 people. It was incorporated in 1880 and had its origins as a European American city. Census records do not give any clarity on how many nonwhite Americans or immigrants lived in the city and how many of them would have been from modern-day India like Mozumdar. However, according to records, there was a population of Asian immigrants brought to help build the transcontinental railroad, and there are twenty-three burials in a section of a cemetery in Pendleton that was reserved for people of Chinese origin. That the people of Pendleton, like the Terpenings, had some prior familiarity with yoga is in line with the idea that certain elements of Asian and South Asian culture were part of the public's consciousness before Mozumdar arrived. And it is likely that Mozumdar, regardless of his personal belief or affirmation in his teachings, adopted a persona that took advantage of how people in America at the time would have thought an Indian spiritual teacher, or guru, to be.

Mozumdar made a career lecturing on a set of his own teachings that he claimed fused Christianity and Hinduism, and science and religion. He codified his teachings in a series of books he wrote and a series of lectures. His lectures were classes that today would likely be labeled "new age" or "self-help." Mozumdar never called himself a guru and even in his writings never called himself a Christian, but he did have all the trappings of a spiritual leader. What we can know about Mozumdar today comes from government records, newspaper articles, his personal writings, and more interestingly, personal accounts, recollections, and memorabilia collected and archived by his followers. Paul Tice, who was a disciple, offers a succinct explanation of his teacher and his involvement in Christian yoga in a 2002 introduction to the second edition of *The Life and the Way*.

"Mozumdar was the founder of the Christian Yoga Society and created a system of thought, or philosophy, for it that is presented in this book," Tice writes. "At first glance it seems that Christian Yoga is a contradiction of terms. Most would believe that systems from the East and West, such as these, are not compatible enough to be enjoined into one metaphysical philosophy but Mozumdar does a masterful job in bridging the gap and bringing them both together. He was a man in touch with the all-embracing God-consciousness—enough to recognize and experience an all-pervading separation and cultural barriers, which is what brought about the creation of the Christian Yoga Society."

Mozumdar published the first edition of *The Life and the Way* in 1911 (through a publisher called the Book Tree) and received positive reviews. "The principal writer is a Hindu of fine intellectual ability and great spiritual zeal intent upon giving a clear message that all things and conditions are according to your concept," Annie Rix Milit wrote in the April–September 1912 issue of *Master Mind Magazine*. "Strong, absolute statements abound in the teachings of AK Mozumdar."

A flier for a six-day lecture series Mozumdar hosted in Chicago (date unknown) advertised day one sessions with titles like "How to Awaken Divinity in Every Part of the Body," "How to Control the Vital Organs, Strengthen Them by Spiritual Means, and Make Them Obey Your Bidding to Perform Their Proper Functions," "How to Control Food Elements," and "The Dominion of the Spiritualized Mind."

Day two sessions included "Projection of Mind," "Mental Vibration," "How to Make Contact with the Souls You Desire to Meet," and "How to Draw Your Comrade Souls." On day three, students learned "Self Education in Sleepland," "How to Function in the Sphere of Master Minds and How to Commune with Them," "How to Develop a Loving Personality," "How to Demonstrate through Love." Day four sessions continued with "How to Reach the Spiritual Realm of Eternal Success," "How to Raise Your Mental Vibration," How to Make Demonstration of All Your

Natural Desires by Never-Failing Spiritual Means," "How to Develop Will Power, Concentration, Memory, and All Natural Talents by Spiritual Means," "How to Control Your Environment and Have Dominion over It," and "How to Solve Your Every Problem." On day five, students learned "How to Insure Permanent Health and Renew and Recharge Your Body by the Use of Cosmic Substance." On the last day, the series ended with "How to Heal Yourself and Others by the Manipulation and Control of Vril Force."

To the modern-day reader, "vril force" most likely has little to no meaning, but in the early 1900s, it was a popular cultural reference, at least among science fiction readers and those interested in the supernatural, from a novel called *Vril: The Power of the Coming Race* by Edward Bulwer-Lytton. (Today, Bulwer-Lytton is probably best known, or unknown, as the writer who wrote the infamous opening line "It was a dark and stormy night.") The fantasy novel *Vril* was about a race of humans, not yet discovered, who would take over the earth with a special ability that allowed them to manipulate a force called vril. Although entirely fictional, vril was co-opted by the Theosophical Society as part of their teachings and would come to represent something that could be attained and used by a group of people who were on the outside of, and better than, society.

Whether Mozumdar read *Vril: The Power of the Coming Race* may never be known. But he used vril and racial language to advertise his teachings and services to would-be followers. "A new race of men," he predicted to his followers, "in control of marvelous spiritual powers through their understanding of the new science of the cosmic ray." Mozumdar used the allure of a new race to further advertise himself. "Do you know that the world is entering upon a new era of startling discovery and achievement? A new super-race is coming to manifestation on this continent?"

"This ray is the very essence of human existence," Mozumdar wrote in another book called *God and Creation*. "It vibrates at the same frequency of the universe, and if we can feel this vibration, we will become a new race of man."

Phrases like "a new race of men" and "a new super-race" are jarring. Read within the context of the modern, post–World War II day, one cannot help but draw parallels between the language on Mozumdar's advertisements and propaganda from Nazi Germany. There are some historical analyses that suggest *Vril: The Power of the Coming Race* was an influence on Nazi ideology. These parallels are speculative at best but at minimum an intent to demonstrate superiority between races, and the promise of being able to better someone's own racial category is apparent in how Mozumdar described and tried to build his community of followers.

It also suggests that Mozumdar saw himself as someone who existed outside the bounds of traditional identity. He is described in a flier advertising his Chicago lectures as "a Christian adept from the land of the Himalayas." Mozumdar was both familiar and foreign. He constructed a sense of himself that was both in the world and out of the world. In what is the only passage I was able to find where he describes himself directly, Mozumdar writes in the introduction of *The Life and the Way*, "The author sends this treatise into the world in the name of the Great Ideal, through whose inspiration he undertook to write it. Excepting the first few pages this book was written inside of a month, in the midst of repeated interruptions by visitors, students, and friends. Without the Divine inspiration and guidance it would have been impossible for the author to write this metaphysics, in the midst of a strenuous, busy life, and in a language which he had acquired in but a short time, by self study."

We cannot know for sure how large Mozumdar's following was, but we can discern from flyers and posters for Mozumdar's classes that they occurred in venues across the United States in cities like Los Angeles, San Jose, Chicago, and Oklahoma City. One reporter covering Mozumdar wrote, "He taught and healed in San Diego, Los Angeles, Seattle, Tacoma, Spokane, Portland, Oakland, Alameda, Milwaukee, Washington D.C., Berkeley, Cincinnati, Chicago, and New York." One flier claimed that Mozumdar's books sold over 50,000 copies. I cannot say I know what Mozumdar's true intentions were with these classes, but he did perform services that would be met with skepticism today. "Public talks will be followed by healing treatments to those who may wish," reads a flier for an event Mozumdar hosted at the local women's club in Burlingame, California. "Love Offering," the flier coyly suggests will be available.

Mozumdar's advertisements included testimonials from members of the American intelligentsia. There was a woman called the Countess Ilya Tolstoy. A *New York Times* wedding announcement affirms she was the daughter-in-law of the Russian author Leo Tolstoy. "Words cannot express my gratitude for what I have received in Mr. Mozumdar's class," her testimonial read. "He is one of the Illuminati whom it is a privilege to contact."

Olive McNeal, the president of a Psychology Club in Washington, DC, called Mozumdar the final word on all spiritual laws. Henry Willington Wack, who presided over the Royal Geographic Society, said in his testimonial, "Mr. Mozumdar and his work is what the world needs today."

Indeed, many of Mozumdar's followers seemed to have some connection to American intellectual or artistic society. "In this way he came into contact with many people who offered their service and their money," wrote journalist Carl A. Anderson in a piece about Mozumdar and his followers.

Mozumdar's teaching was not free. A set of six classes were taught for $50 and sometimes offered at a discount of $35. Using year-over-year inflation rates beginning in 1911, that is the equivalent of approximately $300 per person (not discounted). A set of all twenty-one of his publish books sold for $9.50, or the equivalent of approximately $250 in the present day. His followers had the option to purchase cloth-bound or leather-bound books.

In 1916, the U.S. Census Bureau sent surveys to religious organizations across the country to undertake a census of religious institutions based on self-reported data from religious leaders and their administrators. The resulting 606-page report was called *Religious Bodies* and noted that there were eleven new organizations created since the last census was done in 1906. One of these institutions was Mozumdar's. The Church of the Universal Messianic

Message was listed as having $425 in reported value. This was the equivalent of approximately $10,000 today. The church reported $2,816 in expenditures, or approximately $66,000 today, and no debt. The report also listed the church with having 266 members, 98 men and 168 women.

The team behind *Religious Bodies* describes in their methodology combing through local phonebooks and interviewing local leaders across the country to put together a comprehensive list of religious institutions in the United States. It should be noted that it wasn't until 1974 that the Internal Revenue Service (IRS) started issuing Employer Identification Numbers (EINs). An EIN is essentially a social security number for nonprofit and for-profit companies and businesses. Today, we can use EINs to get an accurate count of companies (including religious organizations), and we can use EINs to understand how religious organizations are incorporated. But the IRS did not hold the same power in Mozumdar's time as it did today. The ability for Congress to levy a national income tax was only ratified with the Sixteenth Amendment three years before Mozumdar's church appeared on a government registry. And even in 1917, the IRS was still promoting advertisements across the country urging people to pay their taxes fully (and on time).

This is all to say that we do not know for sure if the money disclosed in *Religious Bodies* belonged to Mozumdar personally or to his organizations (we don't know if the Church of the Universal Messianic Message was ever formally incorporated). Nevertheless, there are no records of Mozumdar or the church paying taxes. There are also no records of Mozumdar or the church owning land.

In 1919, Mozumdar visited San Bernardino, California. According to an account written by his follower Emma Suydam in 1977, Mozumdar had friends who lived in the mountains. He enjoyed walking along the mountain trails. In another account, Mozumdar liked the area's climate and found "conditions and scenery much like that of his native land." The San Bernardino mountains in Southern California were formed by tectonic activity along the San Andreas Fault with one side lush with forest and lakes and on the other side dusty and dry as the mountains border the Mojave Desert. In the early 1900s, resort towns and camps were built in the San Bernardino forest and alongside its lakes and were becoming popular. It was in a secluded region of forest that overlooked the desert that Mozumdar decided to buy land to build what would eventually become a hundred-acre site called Camp Mozumdar in the present-day city of Crestline. Like immigrants before him and immigrants after him, the opportunity became available for Mozumdar to take a meaningful step in becoming an American. It was time for Mozumdar to buy property.

Mozumdar's experience in the United States was very different compared to many other (mostly) immigrant men who looked just like him and were in the country around the same time. Whereas Mozumdar wore fine tailored robes, was invited to the homes of white neighbors, and charged hundreds and thousands of dollars to sell his image as a "Christian from the Himalayas," other immigrants from South Asia worked as laborers in the country's farms, railroads, and sawmills and struggled to make ends meet in the face of rampant nativism, discrimination, and racism.

In Pendleton, Oregon, the city where Mozumdar is known to have stayed in the home of local couple the Terpenings, lived a journalist named Fred Lockley. Lockley was a popular reporter and writer and in 1907 published an investigative article in the May issue of *Pacific Monthly* that he called "The Hindu Invasion: A New Immigrant Problem."

"Have you ever watched a band of sheep in a rocky and barren field, pastured till the grass has been eaten down to the roots?" Lockley began. "You will see the sheep gather near the fence and look longingly at the luxuriant bunch-grass in the next field, while they march back and forth along the line fence in hope of finding a chance to get into the grassy pasture. Presently some old ewe, her faculties made keen by hunger, will discover a loosened wire where she can wriggle under the barb-wire fence. How long do you suppose it will be, if you do not mend the gap, till the green field is dotted with hungry sheep making the most of their opportunity?"

"India, densely populated, plague smitten, famine-stricken, is that overcrowded and over-pastured field; British Columbia and the United States are the green fields toward which the ever-hungry hordes of India are eagerly looking. They have found the gap and are pouring in. Will the rest follow their leaders in an overwhelming flood? Will India, with her 296,000,000 population, of whom more than 100,000,000 are always on the verge of starvation, become an immigration menace?"

From Lockley's perspective, the "Hindu" sheep were a menace. Around 2,000 had immigrated just north of the border in British Columbia. "If British Columbia is threatened with an invasion of undesirable Asiatic laborers we are vitally interested," wrote Lockley. "Since these Sikhs and Hindus, being British subjects, may enter freely in the United States." By Lockley's reporting, there were 400 Sikh and Hindu men settled in Oregon, Washington, and California. Even though the numbers were small, the threat for Lockley was large. Unlike the Chinese who could be kept out of the country with steep immigration fees ($500 per head), the Sikhs and Hindus were British subjects and thus could not be deterred based on current international relations between the United States and Great Britain.

The "Hindus" also posed a threat to white job security. For the April 1908 issue of *Overland Monthly*, Agnes Foster Buchanan wrote in an article called "The West and the Hindu Invasion," "The Hindus and the Hindu Invasion is the latest racial problem with which we of the West have to deal."

"They have come to this coast eager, more than eager, to do any and all kinds of work," Buchanan continued. "They are to be found in our iron factories, they are picking fruit, railroads engage them as section hands. And right here comes in the problem of cheap labor which is forever and always the same in similar situations. Asiatics are, by their manner of life and living, able to subsist on incomes that would be prohibitive to the white man."

"Then, too, the Hindus have no families to support—that is, there are no women among the new-comers, nor are there likely to be."

"It is just this fact that these men are subjects of Great Britain which makes their right of way into this country more or less an undisputed one. The payment of two dollars head tax and the price of steerage passage out here are all that can keep them, under the present treaty, from swarming over our land."

The story of Mozumdar, taken blindly, makes the case that South Asians, particularly Indians, enjoyed a special relationship with white Americans who wanted, at the turn of the century, services that were of the spiritual variety and, later in the same century, services that were of the scientific. This could not be further from the truth. Lockley and Buchanan were both writing during a period of South Asian immigration that has until only recently been largely forgotten, a period where brown immigrants like "Sikhs and Hindus" were a threat to the American economy and the American way of life.

A short newspaper article from Oregon City, Oregon, published on April 22, 1908 sums up the price many Indian immigrants paid for racial discrimination. Six white men were charged with murdering an Indian man named Harnam Singh. The men "became particularly intoxicated and then came down to the sawmill with guns and taking position behind the cabin of the Hindu, fired shot after shot, until finally one of the bullets struck the unfortunate man." The article ends its description of the harrowing killing with a simple explanation: "Race prejudice was the reason for the action of the men, as several Hindus were employed in the sawmill a few days previous to the shooting."

From the perspective of white Americans, brown men like Harnam Singh were just another set of nonwhite immigrants from Asia. Men like Harnam Singh came to the United States, often via Hong Kong, after hearing about the prospect of good work and wages. They unknowingly followed in the footsteps of immigrants from Asia who were the victims of rampant anti-Asian racism in the United States, beginning as far back as the late 1800s.

By the time Mozumdar arrived in the United States, the phrase "yellow peril" would have been widely known. Found in racist editorial headlines and cartoons in newspapers across the country, the phrase was used to describe the threat Asian men (and it was mostly men who were targeted since they immigrated in larger numbers) posed to American ideals of masculinity, purity, and ultimately whiteness. Asians were seen as dirty and immoral. They brought with them filth and a disregard for maintaining the standards of civic life. These prejudices and racist attitudes were not based on fact but very quickly became institutionalized as the U.S. federal government adopted laws that systemically prevented would-be Asian and South Asian Americans from doing the one thing that had been a staple of an immigrant's adoption of their new homeland—owning land.

When Mozumdar wrote *The Life and the Way* in 1911, American citizenship law limited citizenship to people who were white (a requirement that began in 1792) and who were Black (an extension granted by the Naturalization Act of 1870 that added African Americans after the Civil War). Anybody from modern-day Asia or South Asia—China, Japan, or India, for example—could not become citizens. Additional laws that barely hid their racist intentions by using coded language prevented nonwhite and non-Black people from participating in the basic acts of assimilation and becoming a part of American society. These laws were especially strong in California, Washington, Oregon, Minnesota, Nebraska, Texas, Utah, Wyoming, and Florida. Alien Land Laws prevented undesirables (anybody not white or Black) from owning land and participating in leases. California's Alien Land Law was enacted in 1913 and applied to the property Mozumdar had his eyes on in San Bernardino. The law was updated in 1920 to prevent undesirables from entering into leases and to prevent companies owned by undesirables from purchasing land. (Disturbingly, Florida's Alien Land Law was still in codified legislation in 2018.)

Many so-called undesirables tried to get around the Alien Land Laws. Parents bought homes in the names of their children who were American-born and therefore citizens. The state and federal court systems heard many cases that tried to challenge the constitutionality of the Alien Land Laws in the 1910s and 1920s, but none were successful. Some Japanese and Chinese immigrants even tried to sue for naturalization, hoping that in becoming citizens, they would finally be able to purchase land and fully own their businesses. They were also unsuccessful.

And so, it would be in a country where some white people murdered brown men after a night of drinking, while other white people paid money to hear brown men proselytize, that Akhoy Kumar Mozumdar filed a petition in 1912 to become a U.S. citizen.

4

Where Are You From?

When I was not researching Mozumdar, there were things about life in Seattle I greatly enjoyed: the outdoors, the independent book stores, and the coffee shops. I developed a routine that consisted of weekend hiking trips through Bainbridge Island or Mount Rainier, mornings getting black coffee at Victrola Roasters or Ada's, and evenings spent at the Elliot Bay Book Company looking through their books stacked on pinewood shelves. A day in Seattle and a day in New York are both twenty-four hours long, yet a day in Seattle feels longer. This was a nice departure from my life in the city that never sleeps.

I had a high school English teacher, Mrs. Elwood, who once warned me against leaving New York for another part of the United States. She said, "You don't want to put yourself in a place where people haven't seen someone like you before." I carried this warning with me cross-country, mindful of the irony that to feel like I belonged and to see myself represented in my country's history, I'd have to leave my home in New York and travel to a city where I had no roots. Surprisingly, instead of feeling like an outsider, although Seattle was less diverse than home, I found that I fit in quite nicely. It was Mozumdar I was struggling to relate with.

After buying my copy of *The Life and the Way* from Quest Books, I immediately wrapped it in a book jacket I made from a brown paper bag. The big yellow cross on the book's bright blue cover, juxtaposed against a female figure meditating with her legs lotus-crossed was too much for me. This cover, however, was classic Mozumdar. I could picture in my mind Mozumdar designing it with the goal of attracting the West to a religion of the East. It wasn't Mozumdar's religion that bothered me. It was how he used religion and race, his own religion and race, as a tool to sell an idea of himself to people around him. He peddled language advocating superiority of some races over others. He encouraged stereotypes. He seemed to be assimilated and successful, but he took the path of feeding into the American idea of what he should be. He was whitewashing himself. And here I was expecting a thread of shared Indian American experience connecting his time to mine.

The Life and the Way was not a quick read for me. It took me two weeks, and in that time, I became a regular at a coffee shop that was within walking distance from my apartment in Capitol Hill. One morning, while the coffee beans took a little more time than usual to roast, a blond cashier, dressed in plaid and working the register, started some small talk to pass the time. I asked him if he had any recommendations for places to hear cheap live music. He answered, and then the conversation took a turn.

"So where are you from?" he asked.

"New York City."

"No, where are you actually from?"

Eighty years after Mozumdar filed his petition to become a naturalized citizen in Spokane, I was born in Queens and by birthright became a citizen of the United States.

As a child in Queens, I was acutely aware of citizenship, not because I was ever explicitly told I was a citizen but because there were so many people around me who were not. My parents, for starters, held an immigration status that was somewhat concerning for my five-year-old self: residential alien. They were green card holders, though I never did once see either of them take out a green card from their wallets.

The kids at my elementary school, PS56Q, were mostly brown and not only the children of immigrants but immigrants themselves. In kindergarten we celebrated the Yankees winning the World Series, and we also celebrated each time if one of our parents passed their citizenship exams. For some of my friends, this meant that they were now citizens, too. I learned this in the second grade when Rajindra Prasad left school early and returned the next day to say he had become a citizen. Rajindra had attended his parents' swearing-in ceremony. Once his parents naturalized, their new legal status was conferred to him and all of their minor children.

The day before my parents' own citizenship test, I remember staying up late on a school night with them as they studied last-minute details.

Who wrote the American national anthem? Francis Scott Key.

Who has the power to veto laws? The president.

What is the supreme law of the land? The Constitution.

The image of my parents taking an American civics exam that contained questions I had learned in my social studies class was amusing. I loved being a student and excelled in classes like English and social studies. I remember the disappointment when my mom reported that the examiner had actually skipped all the civics questions and only had her and my dad verify information they had supplied with their application (What is your address? What is your occupation?).

With no tough questions, my parents passed easily. I took the day off school and accompanied them to the Jacob Javits Center, a giant convention center off the West Side Highway in Manhattan, where they were sworn in, waving tiny American flags and reciting an oath alongside thousands of other immigrants.

In my childhood point of view, life with my parents when they were immigrants was no different than life with them as citizens. But citizenship did slowly become a status symbol as more immigrants came to our neighborhood, and my parents joined a new tier of the community that was now older, more settled, and a source of advice for the younger men and women who had more recently moved to the United States. They came to visit my dad to learn how he had navigated the citizenship process. He warned them against unscrupulous attorneys, and they took notes on how to avoid steep legal fees.

My recollections of my parents and friends becoming naturalized citizens are important childhood memories, but in reality, naturalization was so ingrained in New York life that it sometimes felt as common as filing taxes. Yes, naturalization was a difficult milestone that was celebrated, but it was not rare or uncommon. Immigration, and all of its trappings, was just a part of everyday life for me.

The kids in my elementary school were all in the same boat as me. We were Asian, Black, and brown kids who were used to speaking English in school and another language at home. We took for granted that not many of us were citizens, but it was known that eventually we would all become citizens. What was never implicitly assumed was whether we would all become Americans.

This is the paradox. I can only imagine what other immigrants or children of immigrants feel when faced with the question of what happens after citizenship is accomplished. I've already said that life with my parents was no different after they became citizens. Sometimes this felt deliberate, like they were trying hard for things to not change. I noticed the push and pull between my parents' desire for the financial and political stability of being American with the comforting traditions of being Indian. They shunned values and habits they thought were too American: going on vacations, indulging in brand-name purchases, sleepovers, and alcohol. My parents clung to what they thought was Indian: going to temple, observing Hindu holidays, keeping vegetarian, and speaking Hindi at home. It was in my teenage years that this tension between being American and being Indian began to take root in my sense of self and identity. After all, even though I was the child of two Indians, wasn't I only American and nothing else? A person cannot be born in two places at the same time, and yet we can be pulled by the gravity of two different worlds.

Whereas my childhood self took refuge in being surrounded by people who looked like me and experienced the same things as me, my teenage self yearned to become unique and, more importantly, be in control of who I wanted to be. But I quickly learned that others would not understand that I am still American, even when I was vegetarian and I did not go on expensive beach vacations.

When we are born, we are not only given the identity of our birthplace but also the identities we inherit from our parents. It is our job to figure out how to make these identities work for us. Unfortunately, this doesn't happen in a vacuum but in the vicinity of (often) well-meaning opinions formed by people around us.

I am American, but I am some other things, too. On my mom's side, I am Punjabi. On my dad's side, I am Bengali. Along geographic lines, I am also Indian and South Asian. (Interestingly, the term "South Asia," used to describe the area of modern-day Pakistan, Bangladesh, and India, didn't even exist in Mozumdar's time but became popularized in the United States after World War II.) Collectively, these comprise what are the more salient of my identities, Indian American, or South Asian American. I have identities that transcend geography but have also been used to describe who I am. There is the religious, Hindu, even though I am appreciatively agnostic. And then there are the cultural signifiers, Desi (from the Sanskrit word for "land," which has come to describe culture originating from the Indian subcontinent), and the very literal adjective, brown (common today in meme culture on Instagram and TikTok).

Not to risk stereotypes, but there are some parts of me that are distinctly Indian. How I physically appear to other people, for example, or how I enjoy foods with green chilies on the side, or Bollywood movies and bhangra dancing. There are other parts of me that are distinctly not Indian. My love of rock music, tendency to wear all-black clothes, and penchant for coffee are all things that my Indian family might consider too American, or synonymously in the eyes of many nonwhite immigrants, too white. This is where things start to get calculated.

As middle school and high school helped me explore who I was, each one of my interests were classified as either part of my "white" side or my "Indian" side. Each side accrued points as I grew older. If I didn't enjoy Indian classical dance classes, that was one point lost from my Indian side. If I enjoyed reading Indian epics like the *Ramayana*, that was one point won. If I spent afternoons listening to the latest Coldplay album on repeat, that was one point gained for my white side, but every time I went to the beach and risked getting too dark was one point lost. I put constant pressure on myself to keep each side balanced. I agonized over the idea of being "too white" or "not brown enough." The worst thing one of my family or brown friends could accuse me of was being whitewashed.

The adjective "whitewashed" comes from the verb "to whitewash," which literally means to make something whiter with paint. It's used to imply that a person of color has veered far away from their cultural heritage and have instead adopted parts of white, American culture that are not truly their own. The word implies that whoever is whitewashed didn't do enough to understand or be part of their parent's culture. It implies that they changed themselves significantly to be more palatable to the mainstream culture. There's a popular phrase that describes whitewashing in the South Asian community: ABCD, American-Born Confused Desi.

Equal to the risk of being called whitewashed was the risk of being too stereotypically Indian. The phrase "fresh off the boat" is common in many immigrant communities to derogatorily refer to someone who has not yet assimilated to American culture. They retain too much of their home culture's way of life, with the underlying assumption that they are not sophisticated enough to keep up with the (implied) superior nature of American culture.

It's tough to have so many identities, either by choice or by design, and feel like you're not living up to any of them. It's so tough that there's even a young but growing school of psychology that studies the impact immigration has on identity creation among immigrants and children of immigrants in the United States.

I have many moments in my life when I wished that people would look at me and just accept, regardless of my interests, that I am what I say I am. At the end of the day, should what I am even matter? This felt easier in Queens, where everybody looked mostly the same, or at least, my identity was the majority in my community.

When we moved to our white suburb of Long Island, my mom told me that people would always see me as an Indian first and an American second because of the color of my skin. She was right. When you are an American living in the United States and the color of your skin is not white, people assume that you are not from here. They make this assumption just by looking at you. They don't wait to hear what you have to say; they don't wait to get to know you. They look at you, smile, and ask that same loaded question:

"Where are you from?"

I remember waiting in line at the grocery store with my mom, talking about the SATs. We were interrupted by an elderly white man wearing a veterans cap. He told us that he had been stationed in Burma during World War II, that he loved India, and that he was impressed that we spoke English so well. I remember smiling and gently explaining that I was born here and English was my first (and only fluent) language.

It's an odd thing, having to remind other Americans that you, too, are American.

But perhaps it's odder to have to whitewash yourself in order to become recognized as American.

In Mozumdar I hoped to find a figure of American history whose skin was the color of my own and whose actions I could admire. Instead, I found a brown man who could not have known his actions would become history, attempting to prove he was white so he could become an American citizen. Mozumdar was not the first man (and they were always men) given this problematic task. When Mozumdar filed his petition for citizenship in 1912, the American courts system had already ruled on a long line of men of color petitioning to be considered white. The results of their cases constituted a robust set of legal precedents that influenced the outcome of Mozumdar's case. At this point, I had collected a large amount of research on the social and political history of Asian immigration in the United States. What I needed next to understand Mozumdar's case in the context of the United States was the legal history of nonwhite immigrants trying to become American.

5
Defining Whiteness

Whenever I'm asked the question "Where are you from?" I try not to dwell too much on the assumption my questioner is making, that I do not look like what a typical American looks like. I've learned to answer back quickly and politely. I've learned to assume the best intentions in whoever asks it because I know that the United States is a country for everybody, regardless of skin color. I have an optimistic trust that other people either know or are learning to accept this ideal. But I'm not naive to think things were always like this, and that is what I found so shocking about the date of Mozumdar's petition for citizenship. If the United States I live in still struggles with who, based on the color of their skin, is an American, how radical must it have been for a brown person like Mozumdar to claim citizenship in 1912?

To answer this question, I tried to put myself in the shoes of a judge reviewing Mozumdar's case. Just as judges do today, that judge would have had to review materials relevant to the case he was presiding over. I brainstormed ways this could be done and decided to guide my next round of research into reviewing two types of materials: census records and naturalization court cases that dealt with race but also predated Mozumdar's case. My hope was to understand how the United States added and subtracted groups of people to its definition of whiteness. But first I began with trying to find an actual definition for "white" as a racial group.

In 1790, our Constitution was two years old. The founding fathers had moved on from establishing our country as a sovereign nation to governing it. George Washington was president, John Adams was his vice-president, and Thomas Jefferson was his secretary of state. James Madison was a congressman from Virginia, serving in the first United States Congress. All these men were the descendants of immigrants from England. Throughout the thirteen colonies, and into the early years of the United States, England was the number one source of immigration to the United States. Of course, the one notable exception is probably Alexander Hamilton, who immigrated from the British West Indies and whose father was Scottish and whose mother was half-British and half-French (a likely example of what "diversity" might have meant in the eighteenth century).

The Naturalization Act of 1790 limited citizenship to not just people of English descent but also people from other countries whom they thought to be white suggests that the founders had a broad, but not too broad, image in their minds of who could and should be American. The choice to limit citizenship to "white people" allowed our founders to select from a group of people that was large enough to satisfy the need to attract people to grow the country economically but still selective enough to keep the culture in line with what the founders thought to be ideal.

But our founders were not the first to use the word "white" to describe a group of Europeans who were desirable. The word appears in writings in many European languages dating back to the 1600s to differentiate European colonizers from their Black slaves and the indigenous brown people they were colonizing in North and South America. The United States, which was both a colony and a colonizer, was no exception. The Naturalization Act of 1790 was a tool to ensure that the United States and its government would be a country for white people and provided a legal ground to exclude people of color.

When we think about all the ways that we can describe ourselves, or each other, in the present-day, race is the top-of-mind approach. We're asked to check off our race on everything from college applications to social media profiles. But race as a source of personal identity was not common before the nineteenth century. Let's say you asked a hypothetical woman named Marie in 1790 what she was, she said French. Nationality was the primary way people, particularly in Europe, formed their identities. Race, especially race as defined by the color of a person's skin, was not a common idea. Let's say Marie immigrated to the United States and decided she liked her new home enough to become a citizen; upon her naturalization, she would be considered white. And thus, "French" becomes a subgroup of "white" and a part of Marie's identity.

While living in her new home (Marie would have likely settled in the Carolinas, which during colonial times was home to a large French immigrant population. She may have even heard of Paul Revere, whose father was a French immigrant), Marie starts encountering people who look different from her. These are people Marie's ancestors may never have met in their lifetimes. She meets people who are indigenous to North America and have lived on the land for thousands of years before the creation of the United States. She meets people who were taken from their homelands against their will and brought to the United States to become slaves.

Marie, regardless of what she might think or feel toward these people, cannot be equal to the people who are indigenous to North America. This would mean these people who do not look like her have an equal claim to the land that Marie's country has taken. Nor can she be equal to the enslaved people working against their will because they would have an equal claim to the wealth of Marie's country.

The United States used race to differentiate people like Marie from others, and the United States defined race as the color of a person's skin because it was truly the only thing that differentiated Marie from indigenous North Americans and enslaved Africans. Marie might not have had any personal feelings against these people, but she benefited from a government that called her and people who looked like her white. Multiply Marie's experience across the hundreds of millions of white people who arrived and naturalized in the United States over the span of almost four centuries, and you can understand how racism became systemic in American culture and codified in American institutions. To be white was to be desired by the United States. Anything else was undesirable and unwanted by the United States. The main use case of whiteness was to exclude, not to include. The ultimate irony of whiteness as a standard for who could be American is that it could not exist without Blackness, brownness, or any nonwhite "other."

It is not easy to define the other characteristics of whiteness apart from the color of someone's skin in the United States. A familiar refrain I heard from my parents throughout my childhood was that "white" culture in America contained nothing but things borrowed from other cultures or countries. Apple pie was an English invention. Its earliest recipe is from 1381. Rock 'n' roll was a genre of music born out of the musical traditions brought over by enslaved Africans.

For many people who are white, whiteness is valuable and must be protected, whereas for those are not white, whiteness was something to aspire toward. Very literally, in the United States, the Naturalization Act of 1790 made it such that to be white meant that you could belong. And yet, for a country that had designed itself purposefully for the inclusion of only white people, it had a lot of interest in, and a lot of dependency on, colored people.

Every ten years, the United States undergoes a count of how many people reside within its borders. The census, as this decennial civic tradition is called, has occurred without fail since 1790, even during the years of the Civil War. For the amateur history buff or scholar, census records are a treasure trove of information. As the U.S. Census Bureau says for themselves, "the census tells us who we are and where we are going as a nation." Conveniently for anybody with a computer, every census is wholly digitized and accessible online (with the exception of some early census records where raw data were lost in the passage of time). Aside from useful population data, the archive has some fun bits of information that shed light on what life in the United States might have been like at a given time. The 1880 census, for example, included lengthy instructions to census workers reminding them to first and foremost be nice and courteous to everybody they met but to also remember to check the lofts of stables when scouting for dwellings.

The U.S. census is mandated by Article 1, Section 2 of the Constitution, which calls for a population count every ten years to be used to determine how many representatives should be allocated to each state in Congress's House of Representatives. Although the basic requirement for each census is only a population count, every census since 1790 has asked additional questions. Through the years, some questions have come and gone. Citizenship status was added in the nineteenth century and later removed. The census of 1840 asked not just for a count of people in each household but also each individual's occupation, mental health status, physical health, and ability to read and write. The latest census, conducted in 2020, asks none of these questions. The only question that appears consistently in each and every census beginning in 1790, through Mozumdar's time, and into the present day is the question about a person's race. How the census treated race serves as a microcosm for how race was understood in the United States.

In 1790, the first year the race question was held, the census counted the number of free white males aged sixteen or older, the number of free white males aged younger than sixteen, the number of free white females, all other free persons, and enslaved persons. The count of free white males was divided by age to reflect who could vote and who could eventually vote. The count of free white females was not divided by age because women could not vote at all. We no longer have the raw data that would have explained who comprised the group of all other free white persons, but we do know they accounted for 0.02 percent of the total population that was just under 4 million people. Finally, there was the count of enslaved persons. The infamous three-fifths compromise, which can also be found in Article 1, Section 2 of the Constitution, mandated for every five African slaves, only three could be counted toward a state's population for political representation in

Congress and the Electoral College. Of course, African slaves were not allowed to vote at all.

The first set of changes to the race section of the census came in 1820 with the addition of a distinction between slaves and free colored persons. This census asked for a breakdown of free white males by age, a breakdown of free white females by age, a breakdown of male slaves by age, a breakdown of female slaves by age, a breakdown of free male colored persons by age, and a breakdown of free female colored persons by age. This was also the first census to include a question that asked for the count of foreign-born individuals.

The next set of changes came in 1840 with questions that asked for every free white male, free white female, free colored male, free colored female, colored slave male, and colored slave female. The census also asked households for counts of people who were "blind, deaf and dumb, or insane and idiots." (The census used the era's antiquated language for describing disabilities and mental health.)

Up until 1840, the only racial categories that listed in census questionnaires were white or colored. The census of 1850 was the first to introduce a new racial category, "mulatto," used to describe people with one white parent and one black parent. In this same year, "colored" was replaced with the term "Black," making the three racial categories white, Black, and mulatto. The census of 1870 was the first conducted after the Civil War. Slave was no longer a category. The first three categories remained white, Black, and mulatto. Two new racial categories were also introduced. 1870 was the first year indigenous Americans were counted as an explicit racial group called American Indian. This was also the first year people from Asia were counted as part of the catchall term "Chinese."

The race scheme set in the 1870 census persisted until it was updated in 1890 when two new additions were made to describe the race of people with African ancestry. The first was quadroon, used to describe someone who had one grandparent who was Black. The second was octoroon, used to describe someone who had one great-grandparent who was Black. For the time, these were important distinctions. Depending on the state a person lived in, their racial makeup of their ancestry would determine if they were white or Black. The notorious "one-drop rule" had been adopted by many states to mandate that anybody with at least one ancestor who was Black should be considered Black. The 1890 census also added an additional category to describe Asians. Alongside Chinese, a person could also be considered "Japanese." This brought the total set of racial categories to white, Black, mulatto, quadroon, octoroon, Chinese, Japanese, and Indian (again, referring to indigenous Americans).

The final census that occurred before Mozumdar applied for citizenship was the census of 1910. This census contained a race scheme that was far more descriptive than its predecessors and indicated a greater diversity compared to prior years. To start, the question on race listed the racial categories from proceeding years: white, Black, mulatto, Chinese, Japanese, and American Indian. It should be noted that the practice of further grouping people with both Black and white ancestry had been stopped. A person could be white, black, or mulatto. The next racial category to be introduced was "other." Analyzing raw census data from this year reveals that the "other" category captured people from the following backgrounds: Hawaiian, Korean, Filipino, Maori, and Hindu. The year 1910 was the first time someone who looked like Mozumdar was counted in the U.S. census.

I encourage anybody to read through census records between 1790 and 1910. From my reading, a couple of patterns stood out to me and helped me frame the status quo Mozumdar was about to unknowingly subvert. Despite all the changes to the race section of over one hundred years of census questionnaires, "white" as the first racial group remain unchanged. There were some years when a person could list their country of birth or origin. This was likely in response to anti-immigrant sentiment among nativist Americans who were fearful of immigration, even from Europe. But "white" was always the predominant racial category.

African Americans were described many different ways. First, they could only be described as slaves, not for equal political representation or power but to bolster congressional representation for Southern states with the three-fifths compromise. Then they could be classified as either a slave or a free person, with free person becoming the sole classification after the Civil War. The fact that the census went as far as to capture how much of a person's ancestry contained both Black and white parents or grandparents indicates the desire to monitor how much "mixing" was happening between races. It should be noted that it was tremendously difficult, and uncommon, for a person of both white and Black ancestry to be considered white instead of Black.

The census of 1870 is significant in that it was the first census to capture tectonic demographic shifts that resulted with the North winning the Civil War and the abolishment of slavery. The population of the South was drastically reduced as newly freed African Americans began to move northward. The wealth of the South was also drastically reduced when it could no longer count people as property owned by slave owners.

The narratives that dominate this era of American history explain the unique, troubled, and complicated history between white Americans and Black Americans. Historians have dubbed the early nineteenth century as the plantation era, a period when slavery was at its height and contributed greatly to the economies of both the South and the North. What followed was the period of the Civil War in which the North and the South fought for the freedom or continued enslavement of Black Americans. The Civil War gave way to the Reconstruction period, a time when the country struggled between punishing the South and reuniting it with the North. At the heart of this period of American history was the question of whether the United States could live up to its ideal as a country where all men (sexism and a woman's right to vote wouldn't be confronted for another fifty years) could live equally. In reaction to the centuries-old yoke of slavery, historians have, rightly so, dedicated the study of this period to the experiences of Black Americans. The successes of this time, the abolition of slavery and the political empowerment of Black Americans, along with the failures of this time, sharecropping and the rise of the Jim

Crow South, have deep ramifications for how Black Americans and white Americans coexist in the United States today. Modern economic inequalities between Black Americans and white Americans, police brutality of Black Americans at the hands of (often) white Americans, and cultural racism that have made basic truths like "Black Lives Matter" controversial were all born from the seeds planted in this era of history.

There are hundreds and thousands of history books that have been written about the white enslavement of Black Americans and its legacy of racism in the modern United States. Anyone who wants to know more should begin with two books that ought to be required reading for American teenagers across the country. The first is *The Fiery Trial* by Eric Foner. The second is *Race and Reunion* by David W. Blight. These were the first books that I'd read on the subject and ended up being the two books I referred to the most in my research on anything related to race and the United States.

In parallel with this period of American history was also the rise of Asian American history. Race in the United States took on additional dimensions with immigrants from China and Japan. If white Americans struggled to accept a shared country with Black Americans, they equally struggled with these new types of Americans. Newspapers labeled the ancestors of many of modern-day Chinese Americans and Japanese Americans "the yellow peril." Implicit in these writings was the threat these immigrants posed to the purity and whiteness of American society. Although they were not socially accepted and could not be citizens, Chinese and Japanese immigrants were still counted in the census.

With the abolishment of slavery in 1865 with the Thirteenth Amendment, the definition of American citizenship expanded again. The Fourteenth Amendment codified in the Constitution that anybody born in the United States, including slaves, their descendants, and the children of immigrants, were citizens of the United States. The Fourteenth Amendment also codified civil rights in the Constitution by preventing the discrimination of any U.S. citizen, on any basis, by establishing equal protection of all citizens under the law. The Fifteenth Amendment brought down the gauntlet against racist discrimination in 1870 by prohibiting the federal or any state government from denying an American citizen the right to vote based on their "race, color, or previous condition of servitude."

These three amendments laid the foundation for deconstructing government-backed racism and discrimination of nonwhite American citizens. But at the time same, a series of court cases, brought on by Chinese and Japanese immigrants, upheld that these immigrants could not naturalize and become citizens. Through the struggle and change that forced the United States to come to a reckoning with how to expand its definition of American from not just white people but also to Black people, and to the children of immigrants, the Naturalization Act of 1790 still stood untested.

This changed in 1878, when a court in California received a petition for naturalization from a Chinese immigrant named Ah Yup. Petitions for naturalization were not uncommon. Every immigrant seeking naturalization had to submit one to their local court. Petitions contained information about the immigrant that showcased their eligibility for citizenship. This information included how long the person had lived in the United States, testimony from friends, family, or other community members to demonstrate good character, and an assertion that the applicant was racially white. The petition was then submitted to a court officer for review. If the officer had any questions, they would ask the applicant to provide additional materials to their application. If the officer denied an application, the applicant had the ability to bring forth their case to a court judge. As immigrants from Asia increased in the late 1800s, there was an increase in the number of naturalization petitions that were denied by a court officer who thought the applicant was not white. The Ah Yup case was the first of these cases, which would later be called by historians the racial prerequisite cases.

Ah Yup testified in his petition that he was as pale as any white person. On the basis of the color of his skin, Ah Yup was therefore racially white and should be allowed to naturalize as a citizen of the United States. The judge presiding over Ah Yup's case was

Judge Lorenzo Sawyer. Sawyer would become the first of a long line of white male judges who were tasked with deciding whether an immigrant was white or not white. In the case of Ah Yup, Sawyer used the prevailing scientific evidence of the time to determine Ah Yup's race.

Anthropology as a field of study was still nascent. In 1878, a young man named Franz Boas was studying physics at the University of Bonn in Germany. He would later immigrate to the United States (his petition for naturalization was accepted with no issue) and became known by historians as the Father of Modern Anthropology. In 1878, however, he was only twenty years old. Nevertheless, Judge Sawyer used what evidence he had from Boas to determine that Ah Yup, although he was from China, was of a race called the "Mongolian race." The Mongolian race was distinct from the white race, and therefore Ah Yup could not become a citizen. Sawyer's citation of "scientific evidence" would be adopted by two more judges who heard cases of Chinese immigrants attempting to become citizens. "Scientific evidence" became a common reason for courts to deny citizenship to Chinese immigrants whose skin color was just as light as the skin of white Americans. In 1890, a Chinese immigrant named Hong Yen Chang petitioned to become a citizen. His case was denied by a white judge on the basis of scientific evidence. This happened again in 1895 when another white judge denied a petition brought on by a Chinese man.

The Naturalization Act of 1790 gave the American courts system the ability to pick, person by person, who could be considered white and who could not be considered white. For each petition for naturalization received, a court couldn't just declare a person white or not white. The court also had to explain why. This led to a definition of whiteness based not on what whiteness was but what whiteness was not.

In 1898, the Kingdom of Hawaii was overthrown by American businessmen with the help of the American military and annexed to the United States as an American territory. Native Hawaiians had been living alongside Americans who were interested in the islands' resources but went from being an independent people to a group that was deprived of basic rights and citizenship by their new country. Hawaiians could not vote or own property and were governed by officials appointed by the U.S. government in Washington, DC. In the same year, a Hawaiian man named Kanaka Nian petitioned to become a citizen. A white judge dismissed his petition, citing that the same scientific evidence that prevented the Chinese from being white applied to Hawaiians as well.

In 1894, an immigrant from Burma petitioned to become a citizen. This petition was reviewed by a white judge named J. Danaher. In dismissal of the case, Danaher noted that the color of the applicant's skin was a "dark yellow" color. In his opinion, Danaher offered another reason for why a person could not be considered white: "common knowledge." "Common knowledge" became a popular reason for the American courts to deny citizenship on the basis that an applicant was not white. Common knowledge indicated that even though it might be difficult to be explained in words, whiteness was something that was just widely understood within American society.

The next group of people to be racially classified by the American courts were Japanese immigrants. White judges determined that Japanese immigrants were not white but instead "Mongolian" in petitions that were received in 1894, 1902, 1908, and 1910. A white judge declared Mexicans not white in 1897. Another white judge declared any "Native American" not white in 1900.

There were certain groups of people whose petitions for naturalization never were disputed. The English, French, and German, for example, were able to naturalize freely without any question that they could be American. The Irish and the Italians faced discrimination in the United States because they were often Catholic, and not Protestant, but they too were able to naturalize without question. Jewish immigrants also faced discrimination for being a different religion, but they too were ultimately accepted as white. There were, however, some instances where groups of people who would be considered white today were contested. In 1908, a court official denied an immigrant named John Svan's petition for naturalization. John Svan was a resident of Duluth, Minnesota and had immigrated from modern-day Finland. The court official had denied Svan's petition because of a scientific argument of the time that considered Finns to be the descendants of Mongolians. But in this case, the court official had gone too far to narrow the scope of whiteness. A judge named William A. Cant intervened in the case and ruled that John Svan and other Finnish immigrants could be considered white.

By the twentieth century, there seemed to be an understanding within the United States of who was white and who was not. This understanding was particularly important because the twentieth century began to see an increase in the diversity of the American population.

The census of 1910's inclusion of additional nationalities from Asia (the Koreans, the Filipinos) indicates that the government was continually adding to its list of recognized races as new immigrants presented themselves. What puzzled me in reading these records was how arbitrary the government's definition of races seemed to be. In some instances, race was defined by the color of a person's skin, such as the cases of white and Black races. In other instances, it was defined by someone's ancestry, such as in the numerous ways a person of mixed Black and white ancestry would be described. In even more instances, race was described as someone's country of origin, such as with the Chinese and Japanese.

For people like Mozumdar, however, race was described along the lines of religion. The census of 1910 used the term "Hindu" to describe immigrants from modern-day India. "Hindu" is not a race but used to describe anybody who is a follower of Hinduism. Instead, the following words would be used to describe the race of someone like Mozumdar today: South Asian, Asian, Asian Indian, or Indian. None of these words existed in 1910.

Racialization is the process by which a person is assigned a race. Immigrants were racialized, either consciously or unconsciously, as they came to the United States. When a group of people whose racialization did not fit the scheme of white or Black, the U.S. census created and assigned to them a new racial category. That "Hindu" appeared as a race in the 1910 census drives home the point that American definitions of race can be arbitrary, incorrect, and malleable.

In 1909, a man named Bhicaji Balsara petitioned to become a naturalized immigrant in New York. He was part of an Indian ethnic group that emigrated from Persia to India hundreds of years prior. Ethnically, the man was Persian. His religion was Zoroastrianism, but he was light skinned. In his opinion of Balsara's case, a white judge named Ward decided that Balsara's ethnic group was "as distinct from Hindus are the English who dwell in India." Ward granted Balsara citizenship but did not state that immigrants from India were white.

In 1910, a man named Abba Dolla petitioned for citizenship. Dolla was born in Calcutta, like Mozumdar. His parents, however, had emigrated to India from Kabul, Afghanistan. Ethnically, Dolla would be considered Afghani, not Indian. Dolla's petition was denied by the courts but then reheard by a white judge named Pardee (there was a judge named Don Albert Pardee, but I could not confirm it was the same judge who presided over Dolla's petition). Pardee asked Dolla to show his skin to the court. "On being called on to pull up the sleeves of his coat and shirt," Pardee wrote later, "the skin of his arm where it had been protected from the sun and weather by his clothing was found to be several shades lighter than that of his face and hands, and was sufficiently transparent for the blue color of the veins to show very clearly." Dolla's skin color was "sufficiently transparent." He was declared white and allowed to become a U.S. citizen.

In the 1910 census, Balsara and Dolla were not counted as "Hindus" but were instead counted as "others." Had they been counted in the 2020 census, they would have been given greater latitude to describe where they were from, and they most likely would not have identified as white.

When Mozumdar submitted his petition for naturalization in 1913, he did so out of personal choice. He could not have known the arena of race, immigration, and racialization into which he was stepping. When Mozumdar submitted his petition for naturalization in Spokane, Washington, it was initially denied because an examiner saw the color of his skin and declared that he was not white. But Mozumdar appealed, and his case would be the next major case in the line of racial prerequisite cases to determine whether he, and the other "Hindus" like him, could be considered white.

It was now time for Mozumdar, in his own words, to explain to a white judge where he was from.

6

The Difference between Daylight and Darkness

The reality of researching events that happened over one hundred years ago is that sometimes some details are hard to know, such as what Mozumdar wore on his day in court. He could have worn long, flowing robes or a three-piece tailored suit. We do not know if Mozumdar arrived alone, or if he was accompanied by his followers. We do not know what Mozumdar might have thought about testifying that he was white, or what his voice might have sounded like when he spoke.

What we do know is that on May 3, 1913, Akhoy Kumar Mozumdar appeared in court in Washington State's Eastern District to petition for naturalization. We know that at this point, Mozumdar satisfied the residency requirements for citizenship and was determined to be of good moral character. All that remained was to determine whether Mozumdar was white. And for that, Mozumdar spoke directly to the courtroom.

Mozumdar began with where he was born and quickly started explaining, in his own version, his caste. "I come from the northern part of India, from the part of India that customarily spoken of as Upper India, or what is known as Hindustan proper. I am a high-caste Hindu of pure blood, belonging to what is known as the warrior caste, or ruling caste. The pure-blooded Hindus are divided into three castes—the priestly caste, the warrior or ruling caste, and the merchant caste."

"The blood is kept pure by rigid rules of exclusion. Anyone who marries outside of his caste is ostracized, and is disinherited by the native law. None of the high-caste Hindus will have anything to do with him. Marriage outside of the caste not often known." Mozumdar made it a point to illustrate that, like the United States, India had a hierarchy of people. Whereas the American hierarchy was defined by skin color, the Indian hierarchy was defined by caste. And in his hierarchy back home, Mozumdar was at the top.

Mozumdar made sure to differentiate himself from other immigrants who looked like him. "The great bulk of the Hindus in this country are not high-caste Hindus, but are what are called Sikhs, and are of mixed blood. The laboring class, those who do the rough manual labor, are not high-caste Hindus at all, but are in an entirely separate class, having quite a different religion and a different ancestry." By "laboring class" Mozumdar was most likely referring to the turbaned men working the railroads, fields, and lumber yards across the West Coast. This suggests that Mozumdar was very much aware of other immigrants from India and might also have been aware of negative perceptions white Americans had toward them. It would have been to his advantage to set himself apart, and he did so by using a caste-based attempt at explaining racial hierarchy.

"The high-caste Hindus are of Brahmin faith, and in India are clearly distinguished from all of the other inhabitants, including the aborigines of the country, or the hill tribes, and also the descendants of the invaders, those of the Mohammedan faith. The high-caste Hindus always consider themselves members of the Aryan race, and their native term for Hindustan is Aryavarta, which means country or land of the Aryans."

Mozumdar's explanation of where he was from tells us a lot about how he understood the world around him and his place in it. Mozumdar saw himself as better than, if not superior to, other men who were immigrants like him. This superiority, coupled with a pseudoscientific belief that he had an "Aryan" ancestry he shared with Europeans, made Mozumdar argue that he should be considered white.

The man who would decide Mozumdar's whiteness was the forty-seven-year-old Honorable Judge Frank H. Rudkin. He had a long face that ended with a jowl and a large forehead accentuated by a receding hairline. Two years prior, on February 11, 1911, Rudkin took the oath of office to become the U.S. District Court Judge for the Eastern District of Washington.

There is no record or account to suggest that Rudkin had ever met an Indian immigrant before he encountered Mozumdar. It is even less likely that he was familiar at all with the various histories and identities that could possibly constitute the way a person like Mozumdar would see themselves. But Rudkin was tasked with interpreting a law that was, literally, black and white, with no room for shades of color in between.

Rudkin had a reputation for being a fast talker and a sharp thinker. Court reporters he worked with attested to his ability to speak nonstop at over 200 words a minute, much to their dread.

The Eastern District of Washington was a federal court with jurisdiction over several counties in Washington State including Spokane. It was founded in 1905, as the U.S. federal judicial system expanded to accommodate the quickly growing Pacific Northwest.

Rudkin was born in Ohio, studied law at Washington and Lee University in Virginia, and practiced as a private attorney in Washington State. As a young attorney in Ellensburg, Washington, and later North Yakima, Rudkin was a Republican but too new in local politics to begin any sort of career in public life. He attempted to run for a judgeship in 1900, and in July of that year, his winning seemed unlikely. He had been looked over by Republican Party leaders who favored the more experienced Ralph Kauffman of Ellensburg. Nevertheless, Rudkin ran for the position, and by August local reporters declared him the favored candidate for the Superior Court. Rudkin's political career had an unexpected start that year when he was declared the winner of the election on November 8, 1900. He took the oath of office on January 3, 1901 after winning an unquestionable victory.

The types of cases Rudkin heard and ruled varied. In January 1903, he heard a case that called into question whether American courts had jurisdiction over crimes committed on Native American reservations. Rudkin ruled they did not. Later that year, Rudkin ruled that gambling away a lease effectively transferred ownership, even if the lease had not expired or was legally changed. This ruling, local reporters would remark, was an example of Rudkin taking an aggressive approach to interpreting legislation.

Three years after becoming Superior Court judge, Rudkin married Pearl A. Morford. The couple were wed at the home of Frank Sinclair in Yakima on October 7, 1903. They took their vows in front of Reverend H. M. Bartlett. The new Mr. and Mrs. Rudkin left for Seattle on their honeymoon on October 1903. The cases Rudkin took on after dealt coincidentally with marital law. Rudkin disrupted his honeymoon later that month to grant ten divorces in Seattle to couples whose court-appointed judge was absent. "This is a pretty good record for a man on his wedding tour," a reporter commented wryly. Rudkin did not take divorce lightly. He let couples air out their marital problems in court and in one case denied a woman a divorce when he found both she and her husband incorrigible. "The husband was reprimanded, followed by a remark that both ought to be spanked," wrote the court reporter.

Rudkin ran his courtroom staunchly in line with his personal beliefs. He refused to reduce the bail of a rapist and ruled that police courts have the power to fine and convict. His judicial record was impressive enough that by spring 1904, the *Yakima Daily Herald* declared he had an "excellent chance to [be] nominated as one of the supreme court judges" at Washington's State Convention. That year, Rudkin became the Republican nominee for a seat on the Washington State Supreme Court.

But his nomination immediately led to the unearthing of some unsettling events from Rudkin's past. On July 11, 1904, Rudkin was accused of having robbed a man who served as his mentor and benefactor, S. A. Morford, of both his wife and $65,000. The accusation was scandalous and captured the imaginations of newspaper reporters from Washington to California. Rudkin vehemently denied all charges. "I deny every allegation and insinuation of wrong doing made in those papers," he said. Rudkin maintained he had no connection at all to Morford and that the man was lying. But Rudkin's wife, Pearl, had in fact been married to Morford, and by October of that year, the truth emerged. Rudkin had acted as a legal advisor for both S. A. Morford and his then-wife, Pearl, and then presided over their case as a judge and granted the couple a divorce. It was after the divorce that Frank and Pearl married.

In 1905, Rudkin was elected to Washington's supreme court, and he and Pearl began the task of moving to the state capital of Olympia. Fresh from their short-lived scandal, the couple were considered local celebrities by reporters who tracked their public lives. "Judge Rudkin is here to engage in the popular task of house hunting," wrote one reporter for the *Yakima Daily Herald* on the arrival of the Rudkins in Olympia. "Rudkin is no stranger to Olympia, as his acquaintance is state-wide." The reporter accompanied his short article with a photo of Rudkin, in case the reader had not yet had the privilege of ever seeing the judge. The photo, the reporter noted, did not "do him as full justice as he will be expected to join in dispensing, nor does it give a correct impression of his height, which is a full six feet."

Rudkin served on the state supreme court for four years before his name began to float around for an opening on the U.S. Federal District Court. Rudkin tried to remain aloof from the speculation that was following his career. "Personally Rudkin is not anxious for a berth on the federal bench," a reporter from the *Wenatchee Daily World* wrote. "He doubtless would accept an appointment if one were tendered to him." That he wanted the promotion was undeniable. By winter 1910, Rudkin told reporters that he would leave the state supreme court regardless of his appointment to this federal bench, citing his health and that his family no longer wished to live in Olympia. By December 1910, it was revealed in the *Spokane Press* that Rudkin's appointment was being held up for political reasons in Washington, DC. "An inkling has come from Washington as to the reason for the delay in the appointment of the federal judge for this district," a reporter wrote. "The arguments used against Rudkin consist of some of the things brought out in the recent supreme court campaign." In 1911, Rudkin's appointment to the federal bench was approved, but his career remained in flux. On the advice of his friends who pointed out that Rudkin had been elected by the people of the state of Washington to serve six years on the state court, Rudkin decided he would not resign and instead see his term to completion.

Rudkin turned down President William Howard Taft's appointment, but Taft would have none of it. A reporter for the *Seattle Republican* explained Taft's feelings toward Rudkin as such: "Judge Rudkin on the State Supreme Court Bench is considered one of the strongest legal minds that ever occupied that position. . . . Whether a private citizen, or a superior court judge, or a chief justice of the state supreme court he has always been Frank H. Rudkin and success has never made him any more than he always assumed to be."

Once Rudkin eventually accepted Taft's nomination, he was confirmed by the U.S. Senate. The *Seattle Republican* reported on his assuming the federal judicial seat and hinted that this would not be the last nomination (or promotion) for Rudkin.

"Frank H. Rudkin took the oath of office last Saturday," the article read on Friday, February 17, 1911, in a quaint reminder that news wasn't always delivered in a timely fashion at the turn of the century. "It is said by those who seem to know whereof they speak that Judge Rudkin will be heard from again along the line of judicial promotion."

The newspapers kept an eye on Rudkin's career and covered any cases that were of public interest. In 1912, the *Newport Miner* ran a front-page story (above the fold) on a dispute Rudkin settled between two rival telephone companies. Later that year, in March, Rudkin appeared again on the front page (also above the fold) of the *Tacoma Times* in an article that reported Rudkin being accused of bias during jury selection for a census fraud case.

History buffs and historians alike will appreciate that the Library of Congress maintains a digitized archive of American newspapers between 1789 and 1963. The archive can be browsed by year or by publisher for those interested in meandering through old headlines and advertisements. The archive can also be searched by keywords for those with a more specific subject in mind.

Newspapers are a helpful and fascinating tool to understanding the past. Newspaper articles offer depictions of events that do not benefit from the hindsight that comes with writing with the time to reflect on what happened. They reflect what was important to people in a community at a period of time. They reflect how people spoke and thought about the world around them. It's not just the articles published in historic newspapers that are interesting but also the articles that are not published. Events or facts or ideas that don't pass an editor's final read before sending an edition to the printer get lost in history, or are discovered later, making their initial absence speak volumes.

With Mozumdar's case making national headlines, the newspapers put Rudkin on the map. "Is a High Caste Hindu a White Man?" read the headline that appeared in the March 12, 1913 morning edition of the *Weekly Journal-Miner*. "Realizing that the decision in this case will be one of the most momentous a western judge has been called upon to make and will rank with the noted decision of a federal judge that Finns are not Mongolians and are entitled to citizenship. Judge Rudkin declared that he would have to take the case under advisement."

Reading Rudkin's writing about Mozumdar's case, over one hundred years later, it is very odd for me to think that a judge could have looked at an Indian man, whose skin was likely the same color as mine, and ask if that man was white. I also have trouble imagining myself, a brown Indian woman, claiming to be white. As far as one's race is defined by the color of one's skin, identification is often pretty unquestionable. There are instances of *passing* (where a person can get away with identifying with another race because of their skin color), of course, but to claim to be one race while very clearly being another seems wrong. Rudkin likely saw the same difficulty but perhaps in a different lens.

"The difference between daylight and darkness is apparent to all," he wrote, "but where is the dividing line, and where does daylight end or darkness begin? So it is with the races of mankind, where miscegenation has been in progress for generations."

I picture Mozumdar and Rudkin facing each other from opposite sides of a courtroom. Like in a courtroom drama, Rudkin sits behind his judicial bench, slightly raised above everybody else. Mozumdar stands behind a witness stand, making his case. On one side, a brown man who immigrated to the United States. On the other side, a white man who was the son of immigrants. But these two men were not very different. After all, Mozumdar did not only petition to be a citizen of the United States; he also petitioned to be a white man. And Rudkin never once questioned the constitutionality of the white clause for citizenship.

There could not have been any other path to citizenship. In his opinion of Mozumdar's case, Rudkin investigated what he believed to be our founding fathers' intent with the Naturalization Act of 1790's white clause. Rudkin does not mince words.

"In the original Naturalization Act," he wrote, "the expression 'free white persons' was doubtless primarily intended to include the white emigrants from Northern Europe, with whom the Congress of that day was familiar, and to exclude Indians and persons of African descent or nativity."

Rudkin then turned a more charitable lens on the founders' next. "Beyond this, perhaps, Congress had no definite object in view. It could not have foreseen the vast immigration problems with which the government is now confronted, or the difficulties which might hamper and embarrass the courts in the administration of the law."

"But, whatever the original intent may have been, it is now settled, by the great weight of authority, at least, that it was the intention of Congress to confer the privilege of naturalization upon members of the Caucasian race only."

In an attempt to fact-check Mozumdar, Rudkin relied not on the accounts of another Indian but rather on the account of a (white) psychologist who had visited India and happened to be a Frenchman, Gustave Le Bon. Interestingly, Le Bon would become influential and better known for his early writings on the psychological phenomenon of group think. But in 1905, he contributed to an encyclopedia called *Great Events by Great Historians*. His contribution outlined the creation of the caste system in India. Riddled with inaccuracies, this text was nevertheless cited by Rudkin in his judicial opinion.

Of India, Le Bon wrote, "The number of individuals white enough to prove that their blood is quite pure is very restricted." Rudkin had decided that in order for Mozumdar to be white, he had to prove he was a pure-blooded Brahmin, that the Brahmins were descendants from the Aryans, and that the Aryans were the Caucasian race.

When immigrants come to the United States, the nuance of where they are from is often designed to suit the needs of a given moment. I've been guilty of this myself. I stubbornly say I'm from New York, when I know that whoever is asking me the question wants me to confirm that I'm from India because that is their assumption after looking at me. Self-identity is not something immigrants have full control over. Racial identity, ethnic identity, even religious identity, are all things that can be assumed and judged externally. They are also all things that can be juggled in multiple versions.

Mozumdar was simultaneously many things. He was a high-caste Hindu Brahmin priest. Born in Calcutta, he was from India, which he chose to define as Aryavarta. But Mozumdar was also a Christian yogi from the land of the Himalayas. Mozumdar was brown, just like the workers who also came from India across the Pacific. But he was also white because unlike those workers, he was of a different caste.

When Rudkin later summarized the proceedings of Mozumdar's naturalization case, he was able to capture Mozumdar's testimony and background and his own research in just a little more than 1,000 words. I have struggled unpacking all of the history of a single individual and his country from Mozumdar's short testimony. Mozumdar was very likely sharing a version of the history of his identity that he was taught to believe. And Rudkin was very likely hearing a version of history that he was primed to accept. Today, we have access to genealogical research that suggest that there was no such thing as an "Aryan migration," or an "Aryan race" for that matter. We have the hindsight of the dangerous consequences and fallacies behind attempting to define one group of people superior to another. Perhaps Rudkin was aware of his own limitations, having to decide Mozumdar's race in the context of his time.

"I fully appreciate," Rudkin wrote in the final moments of his deliberation, "the fact that the lineage of the applicant in these matters must rest largely, if not entirely, upon his own testimony, and that the courts may be imposed upon." But this limitation did not stop Rudkin from making his decision. Frank H. Rudkin granted Akhoy Kumar Mozumdar citizenship on May 3, 1913. Mozumdar was officially a white man.

The newspapers were the first to react.

7

The Dilemma

From Monday, May 4, 1913 through the rest of the week, Americans around the country awoke to headlines about the man with a strange name from Washington State.

HINDU BECOMES AMERICAN.
THE FIRST HINDU TO BE MADE A CITIZEN.
HINDU ADMITTED TO CITIZENSHIP.

Newspapers in the 1900s were in their golden age. The powerhouse newsrooms, which would give rise to the Hearst Magazine empire and the Pulitzer Prize in a couple decades' time, were all located on the East Coast. The American West was riddled with local newspapers, with circulations in the thousands and hundreds of thousands that serviced small towns and big cities alike. There were so many newspapers in print that readers could find the paper that openly supported their political beliefs, however niche, or the paper published in their native language (German-language newspapers were particularly popular).

News traveled relatively quickly. Newspapers shared with each other articles and headlines. If a breaking news event was reported in a Salt Lake City newspaper, all a Boston editor had to do was rerun the exact article and headline in his (and at this time, all known newspaper editors were men) own paper. This was also the time of the flourishing newswire services. Once the Associated Press picked up a story, it would quickly find its way to newsrooms across the country. And so, it took only one day for news of Mozumdar's citizenship to leave Spokane and travel east to appear in Washington, DC's *Evening Star*, stopping in multiple cities along the way. The first cities to pick up the news were in the American West. The *Las Vegas* (of New Mexico, not Nevada) *Optic* made Mozumdar its cover story. The *Santa Fe New Mexican* ran Mozumdar's story on page two, alongside its section on "society notes," updates from the local high school, and an advertisement for the latest fashion from Paris—pockets for women. The *Daily Capital Journal*, in Salem, Oregon, called Mozumdar's citizenship "an interesting sidelight on the anti-alien land legislation in California," referring to the popular policy of denying land-ownership rights to people who were not citizens (in an effort to curtail the assimilation of people from modern-day Asia and South Asia). Mozumdar's news traveled on to front page of the *Ogden Standard* of Ogden City, Utah and to the front page of the Sunday edition of the *Omaha Daily Bee* in Nebraska. News of the first brown Hindu to become a "free white person" and citizen reached newspapers in Bismarck, North Dakota, Birmingham, Alabama, Norwich, Connecticut, and Albuquerque, New Mexico. In Texas, the *Amarillo Daily News* added a punchline to its reporting: "Akhay [sic] Kumar Mozumdar, a high-caste Hindu, has been made a full-fledged American citizen. All right, but we favor changing his monaker [sic] to Smith." News traveled next to Libby, Montana, Marshall, Missouri, Bonners Ferry, Idaho, and finally, left the continental United States to appear on the second page of the *Honolulu Star-Bulletin* in Hawaii. Mozumdar's case was even translated to German and Finnish foreign-language newspapers.

Mozumdar's citizenship was of particular interest to members of the West Coast's class of politicians, wealthy landowners, and public thinkers. Rudkin's decision that Mozumdar was a white man created a legal precedent in the American courts system that threatened to upset the delicate tactics state governments in California, Oregon, and Washington used to prevent people of Asian nationalities from owning land.

By 1913, California, Oregon, and Washington State, in addition to other states, passed a series of acts called the Alien Laws. These laws were designed to prevent people of Asian descent from purchasing property. Racist and xenophobic state congressmen (and they were all men) sought to appeal to white voters who were worried that they would be forced to become neighbors with men and women from modern-day China, Japan, Korea, and India. The immigrant population, particularly from China and Japan, was rapidly growing along the Pacific Coast, and with this growth came the perceived threat to a white, American way of life.

These Alien Land Laws created tensions not just between white Americans and Asian Americans trying to live side by side but also on the global diplomatic stage. President Woodrow Wilson was trying to maintain friendly diplomatic relations with Japan, a necessary partner for trade across the Pacific Ocean, which had become increasingly important to the American economy with the opening of the Panama Canal and faster transport from North America to Asia. In order to create amenable trade relationships with Japan, the United States signed and agreed to the treaty of 1894 with Japan, which stated that the United States would guarantee to Japanese subjects living in the United States "rights of residence, and privileges in accordance with Japan's status as a most favored nation."

And so, opponents of the Alien Land Laws argued that it was unconstitutional because as state laws, they violated federal treaties. While the constitutionality of the Alien Land Laws was debated in courts, Mozumdar's case threatened to deal another below. Years before, the California Supreme Court, when ruling on whether people from China were able to own land, issued the opinion that people from China were of the same ethnicity as people from India. Mozumdar's case, which was decided in Washington State, therefore had implications for the citizenship of Chinese immigrants in California. Furthermore, if Chinese immigrants could now be considered high-caste Hindus and therefore be white, this could also be applied to Japanese immigrants and thereby nullifying the Alien Land Laws.

Researching this history in the present day is confusing. Even people living during this time period were puzzled. Different courts in different states had different rulings about what people from Asia ethnically were. Different courts in different states also had different rulings about what these people could and could not do. Mozumdar's case was the first of its kind where someone who was most definitely not white, from a part of the world that was not known to produce any ethnically white people, had been ruled by an American court as white.

Charles E. George, the publisher of a trade publication based in San Francisco called the *Lawyer and Banker*, put it succinctly in an editorial that ran in newspapers throughout the summer of 1913 and across the country: "It is a dilemma," he wrote, "from which there appears to be no escape."

Aside from the *Amarillo Daily News'* short quip that they would prefer Mozumdar change his last name to something that sounded more American, there is not much evidence from newspapers and writings of the time that there was any racial or ethnically motivated negativity toward Mozumdar personally. The coverage of Mozumdar's case appears to be less about Mozumdar himself and more about the confusing state of American naturalization laws at the time. What was clear from Mozumdar's case was that the laws were not properly enforcing who could be American and who could not.

In 1913, the tallest building west of the Mississippi was the twenty-one-story Call Building in downtown San Francisco. The Call Building was home to the *San Francisco Call*, one of the more prestigious newspapers that catered to West Coast intelligentsia. The *Call* covered Mozumdar's case carefully.

On May 6, two days after news of Mozumdar's case broke, W. W. Chapin, the *Call*'s publisher, wrote, "This very interesting decision raises the subject of naturalization in general and the need of a federal law which shall saw explicitly and without evasion just who may or may not become American citizens."

Chapin went on to warn against the American courts being tasked with classifying different groups of people by race: "The idea of resting citizenship upon the casual interpretation of a disputed ethnological question when ethnology itself is not an exact science, and the interpretation is made by a man who is not an ethnologist, is to say the least, almost a logical reduction to an absurdity."

"But the naturalization laws," Chapin concluded, "will be an absurdity until they are made clear, exact and precise." In the meantime, "under Judge Rudkin's decision that a Bengalee [*sic*] may become a citizen there is likely to be an influx from that presidency, as Calcutta is its capital, access to the coast is easy, and that one presidency alone has a population of more than 50,000,000 people."

Chapin's warning was quiet but clear. Now that Mozumdar was white, a citizen, and entitled to all the rights that came with citizenship such as land ownership, there was little local governments could do to prevent other immigrants from Asia from becoming citizens. And as for the other men and women who were brown like Mozumdar, well, there were now at least 50 million of them who could now come to the United States, become citizens, and alter the portrait of American society forever.

I am a descendent of the 50 million people living in Calcutta in the very early days of the twentieth century. Reading the words of Chapin and George is a cold reminder that before Mozumdar, people who looked like me could not vote or own property because the United States did not think brown people from India could become citizens.

Before I started writing this book in 2015, I was a reporter at ABC News. I covered breaking news events, and from 2014 to 2015, Black Lives Matter, the shooting of Trayvon Martin, and the racial discourse that led to the nomination of Donald Trump as the Republican candidate for president dominated my headlines. All of these events were erupting out of the legacy and unfinished work of the hundreds of years of civil rights activism led by African American leaders like Frederick Douglass, Sojourner Truth, Malcolm X, and Dr. Martin Luther King Jr. At this time, I lived in Harlem, New York, where it was impossible to forget the active work of civil rights in this country.

And yet, I didn't really consider Mozumdar's story as that of a civil rights struggle for South Asian civil rights. Maybe it's because South Asian civil rights in the United States were not born out of civil rights marches. There were no impassioned speeches or boycotts or peaceful protests. Instead, we had one man who unwittingly found himself in a moment in time that would become a lasting piece of history. All Mozumdar wanted, really, was what most immigrants in the United States want: he wanted to own land.

After Mozumdar became white, he was able to bypass the Alien Land Laws as a citizen and purchase his acres of land in San Bernardino, California. On this land he built Camp Mozumdar. He built a large, white, domed temple. He built an amphitheater. And he built a home for himself and his followers. Mozumdar never married, and he never had any children. But Camp Mozumdar exists today, and it can be seen from Mozumdar Drive, which is now a residential street in the hills of San Bernardino.

There is, in Mozumdar's story, an opportunism that is uniquely American. Mozumdar created for himself an identity that could not really exist anywhere else in the world except in the United States. He sold and profited from this identity in a manner that brought him great wealth. He used that wealth to build monuments to his name. In this way, Mozumdar was just like many other Americans before and after him.

I don't know if Mozumdar saw his becoming white as a victory for anybody other than himself. Historians are supposed to keep their feelings about their subjects separate from their documentation of their subjects. I'm not a historian, and Mozumdar's story is deeply personal. Mozumdar was likely driven more by his individual needs than by perceived injustices that were being brought onto people like him. Mozumdar was not trying to fight for South Asians to become citizens. He was not trying to prove the fallacy of the United States' requirement that all citizens be white. He was just trying to become a citizen.

On May 6, the same week he received his citizenship papers, Mozumdar traveled to Oakland, California. In Oakland, he was the guest of a local "yoga congregation," as reported by the *San*

Francisco Call. During his visit, he must have been asked to comment on the nationwide reaction to his citizenship because the *Call* goes on to reprint Mozumdar's only statements on record of his citizenship. "The Hindu will never form a serious immigration problem for the United States," Mozumdar is reported to have said. "For the reason that the high caste Hindu never leaves his native country and the coolie class have no means of coming here, as well as being debarred as unskilled labor without means."

Of course, Mozumdar was wrong.

Now that Indians were white, many applied for citizenship to the United States. Some of these people were actually high-caste Hindus. For ten years, between 1913 and 1923, these people, primarily in California, immigrated, became citizens, purchased property, built businesses, started families, and even made nationwide headlines for plotting to overthrow the British government. The American courts had no choice but to observe Rudkin's precedent: Indians were white. All the while, the American government watched silently and with concern as it observed this growing group of brown men and women become Americans and challenging for the first time the Anglo-Saxon ideals of American citizenship.

Indian American citizens were the subject of surveillance of law enforcement. They were written about in local newspapers and had their lives documented by immigration officers. They were studied by academics and ethnographers, who were curious about this new type of American who were not winning any favors with public opinion (the term "model minority" had not been coined yet, and there was nothing "model" in how these new Americans were viewed by the public). All of this produced a treasure trove of history that today can be found in the largest collection of preserved primary source materials about South Asian Americans.

To learn who these people were and the tragedy that would befall them in 1923, I would need to visit this collection. In 2016, my journey took me from Seattle to the Bancroft Library in Berkeley, California.

A promotional photo of Akhoy Kumar Mozumdar, taken for one of his early promotional tours through the United States in 1909.

Akhoy Kumar Mozumdar, pictured center right, stands with his followers sometime between 1911 and 1918.

Bhagat Singh Thind enlisted in the U.S. Army in 1918 and is pictured here in his military uniform in Camp Lewis, Washington State.

Bhagat Singh Thind was the first South Asian American to serve in the U.S. military. He is pictured with the rest of Camp Lewis in 1918.

Kala Bagai was featured in the *San Francisco Call* when she first immigrated to San Francisco with her family. This photo and article were published September 17, 1915.

Kala Bagai photographed wearing a sari the year she immigrated to the United States in 1915. She was twenty-two years old.

Kala Bagai photographed with her husband, Vaishno Das Bagai, and their sons in San Francisco in 1921.

Judge Frank H. Rudkin, pictured here in 1910, declared that Mozumdar was white and therefore eligible for citizenship.

Associate Justice George Sutherland overturned lower courts' decision that South Asians were white. His decision led to the denaturalization of some South Asian Americans.

JJ Singh, pictured third from right, watches as President Harry Truman signs the Luce-Celler Act, granting citizenship to South Asian immigrants in 1946.

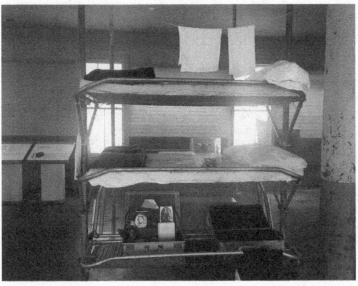

Immigrants waiting to enter the country slept on sparsely furnished barracks.

Angel Island Immigration Station, as it can be seen from the trail from Angel Island State Park.

The immigration station has been reconstructed from the outside, with the original building maintained inside.

Ships carrying immigrants to Angel Island stopped at this cove and were often docked for months before passengers were allowed to disembark.

An article in the *San Francisco Call* announces Mozumdar's successful petition for citizenship in 1913. Historical newspapers are available for free on the Library of Congress's digital archives.

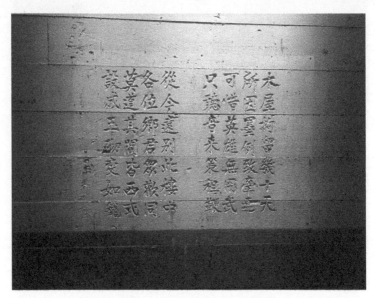

Immigrants were detained for so long that many etched personal stories, letters to home, and pleas to enter the United States on the walls. These etchings have been preserved and can be viewed today.

Angel Island, pictured here in 1935.

8

Return to Hindoo Alley

Exactly one hundred years after Mozumdar arrived in Seattle, Washington aboard the *Empress of China*, I was a seventh grader in Roslyn Middle School in a social studies class with a teacher curiously named Mr. Best (to this day, I'm not sure if this was his real name or assumed name, and have left it unchanged). Mr. Best didn't just have an unusual name but also an unusual teaching style. His students did not take any exams. Instead, we had to write papers after every lesson discussing whether we agreed with the actions of a figure of American history.

Mr. Best taught history as if it was a story and constantly reminded us that all good stories carry a different weight when they are based on real events. Life always had a way of being stranger than fiction. And unlike fiction, life, and therefore history, had a way of not always delivering a happy ending. Mr. Best instilled in us that the great figures of history were people, just like us. They were not characters with redemption arcs or last-minute change of hearts that gave them the proclivity to do the right thing. They made mistakes, just like you and I have. Sometimes they were ordinary people forced to live in extraordinary circumstances. And some of them, the truly great ones, lived by the idea that their actions mattered to future generations.

The bottom line, according to Mr. Best, was that we shouldn't idolize or glorify the people whose stories comprised American history. They were not larger than life; they were human. Their humanity was important to keep in mind when studying their choices and actions.

After we completed our unit on the American Revolution, Mr. Best assigned our first paper that had an air of controversy. We had to write whether we believed, after learning that founding fathers like George Washington and Thomas Jefferson profited from slavery in the colonies at a time when the British abolitionist movement was gaining traction among British society and Parliament, that the founding founders were freedom fighters who genuinely believed in liberty for all people or opportunists who sought to protect the American slave economy. The idea that Washington could be anything but the upstanding hero of freedom we were taught to see him as was shocking. I'm pretty sure at least one parent called our school to complain. But Mr. Best defended himself simply that we were free to agree or disagree as long as we defended our point of view with facts.

For our group of twelve-year-olds, facts came from a series of books we were assigned to read that year called *A History of US* by a woman named Joy Hakim. Like me, Joy Hakim was born in Queens, New York (Forest Hills, to be exact). And she was the first academic and author I noticed who seemed to have made for herself a successful career writing books about history. That she was also a female author did not escape me. (Today, her *A History of US* is still one of the best-selling book series about American history. If you're reading this book and you've made it this far, chances are you'll really enjoy *A History of US*, too.)

A History of US was popular with my classmates for two reasons. First, these books were light and in paperback. Each book (there were ten, each about a different period of American history) was at most 150 pages and filled with color photographs, portraits, maps, and images of artifacts. They were much easier to carry around than the stuffy, hardcover, thousand-page textbooks we were accustomed to carrying in our backpacks like a pile of bricks. For a child, this was a huge selling point.

The second reason for *A History of US*'s popularity was its series title. It's a clever pun between an abbreviation of the United States and "us," as in "all of us." As soon as we realized this, we all thought we were privy to an insider's look at our country's history. More importantly, we were privy to our history. We were all part of the American community and this was our shared history. This was the story of us.

I loved the sentiment, but as a twelve-year-old Indian girl who was the only brown kid and child of immigrants in my predominantly white, seventh-grade social studies class, I didn't buy into this sentimental notion of inclusion. Nowhere in the books of *A History of US* were pictures or photographs of someone who looked like me. There were some women, like the female colonists of Massachusetts during the Salem witch trials, and a pair of Black women living in the United States before the Civil War who won a legal battle that integrated street cars. But there wasn't a single person from India that I can recall. As an Indian American girl reading these stories about mostly white men, I hoped for inclusion. I was disappointed. *A History of US* felt more like a history of "them."

I wasn't exactly surprised. At the time, I was taught to believe what most people probably believed that South Asian American history began in the 1960s. I couldn't expect to see people from India, Pakistan, or Bangladesh in American history books that were about America before the modern period. So if you were writing a book about South Asians in America at the turn of the twentieth century, for example, there couldn't *possibly* be any South Asians to write about.

My twelve-year-old self simply assumed that South Asian American history was still being lived. It hadn't reached a point where it could be documented.

I don't know if other children of immigrants have ever felt this way, but for me, the lack of representation (and representation was not a word I would have known to use in 2005, but looking back, this is exactly what I needed) in American history made me acutely aware that my actions would make up the early history of my community in the United States. In my childhood imagination, I pictured future generations reading about me and brown people at the turn of the twenty-first century the way we read about Eastern European immigrants at the turn of the nineteenth century.

Couple this imagination with typical middle school existential angst and often being the first (and only) brown girl whom white people around me met on Long Island, I felt enormous pressure to live in a way I would be proud to read in a history book. There were no brown people as heroes, villains, or a mixture of both in any of my history books. Leading lives that were complicated, individualistic, or self-serving was not a luxury I could have.

My purpose was seemingly clear. I had a responsibility to get into a good school, study law, become an attorney, and make an income that could give me a stable, safe, and predicable life. This was a life handed to me because, as the child of immigrants who had risked everything to come to the United States, I had a duty to turn that risk into reward.

I had to be polite and unassuming. I had to be proud of everything that made me different, but I could not call too much attention to myself. I had to blend in. I couldn't upset my surroundings. Making ripples or waves wasn't just not unexpected; it was not allowed. I had to be perfect. By virtue of being South Asian, I was representing South Asians to people who had never met South Asians before. Any flaw or mistake wasn't just a reflection of myself; it was a reflection of my community. To be anything but a perfect "model minority" was impossible. I had no role models for anything else.

Although I didn't realize it at the time, as there was virtually nobody with whom I could share these thoughts, my experience and feelings were shared by other immigrants and children of immigrants. I was reminded of this feeling years later when I read Mozumdar called other South Asian immigrants "coolies" in the *San Francisco Call*. Mozumdar was not perfect; he was complicated. He used a racial slur against his own people. He was never a reflection of his community; he eschewed his community. Even his contribution to South Asian American history, the right to citizenship, was motivated by his own self-interest. I'd never heard the word "coolie" before, which was probably for the best as it is wildly offensive. (The British called Mohandas Gandhi this slur in his early days as a lawyer in South Africa.) A Google search for the word took me to the *Oxford English Dictionary's* very succinct definition: "an offensive word for a worker in Eastern countries with no special skills or training." The slur originated in India by white Europeans who used it to describe day and migrant laborers. These laborers constituted the lower rungs of Indian society who were, along with their families, coerced into indentured servitude by Europeans, in particular the Portuguese and the British, and traded around the world to colonies in Southeast Asia, Africa, the Caribbean, and South America. These people were slaves in everything but name. Indentured servitude is a fancy way to say slave and that's what these people were. They were enslaved. The etymological history of the slur dates back to the Sanskrit word for slave. Even after winning their freedom generations later, these people were treated as second-class citizens in their adopted homelands.

Beginning in the 1800s, Americans adopted the word "coolie" to describe immigrants coming not just from India but also China, Japan, and all other parts of Asia. Coolies were the opposite of white Americans. According to stereotype, they were dark, dirty, and uneducated. They were capable of living in squalor and not the means or inclination to be anything but destitute. Coolies posed a threat to society by bringing with them filth and iniquity. By Mozumdar's time in the United States, the slur had become synonymous with anybody from Asia or of Asian heritage.

That Mozumdar used this word to refer to other Indian immigrants is telling. It suggests that although an average white American living on the West Coast in 1905 might not have seen a difference between Mozumdar and another immigrant with brown skin, Mozumdar certainly felt he was different. He created a life for himself in the United States that was predominantly white. There is little to no evidence of Mozumdar interacting at all with other brown people. I cannot say with certainty how he related to other South Asian immigrants in the United States at the same time as him, but it's almost certainly true that he did not think he himself was a coolie. Mozumdar believed he was a white man. He just so happened to establish a precedent that dictated that people like him, coolie or not, were also white.

There is a tendency within minority communities in the United States to forget just how disparate and discordant people in these communities can be with each other. Consider the term "South Asian." I use it in this book to describe myself, Mozumdar, and other characters who are from or descend from the region of modern-day Pakistan, India, and Bangladesh. It's a term used throughout the United States today to describe not just Pakistani Americans, Indian Americans, Bangladeshi Americans, but anybody from South Asia. But it's not a term used in South Asia to describe a shared heritage or culture. At most, it's a geographic signifier and not a descriptor of identity. (The U.S. State Department first coined the term "South Asia" during World War II, wrongly ignoring the historical and distinct regional differences that made this part of Asia so diverse.) To be South Asian American is to trade differences for a strength in numbers that combines populations from India, Pakistan, and Bangladesh and other South Asian countries who now live in the United States. The cost of political strength is a homogeneity that just isn't true.

People on the inside are just as guilty as people on the outside in making this push for sameness. If you are a member of a minority community, you receive countless stereotypical subliminal (and not so subliminal) messages from people outside of your community about who you should be or how you should act. You also receive a proportional, if not more, amount of pressure from people within your own community about how you should be or how you should act. And without proper representation in the places we study or work, our governments, our culture, and certainly our history, living with this pressure can be difficult.

Without seeing themselves represented in what they want to do or spaces they want to occupy, people of color have to choose to become "the first" of their community to do something. To be "the first" brings with it the added burden of needing to represent not just yourself but others like you. If you succeed, it is in spite of the institutional systems that are designed to keep you out and the community-built systems that don't know how to support you. If you fail, you've inadvertently deterred others like you from following.

This is an inherent tension around immigrant life in the United States. On the one hand, we're used to being "the firsts." The will-power and conviction to be an immigrant is not one that always requires someone to have seen somebody immigrate before them. With immigration often comes a fresh start. To be somewhere where there is no one like you is empowering. You are decoupled from the past and any stereotypes about you. And yet, for immigrants in their new country, and for their children, the same thing that is empowering can also be stifling. Without representation, which is the ability to follow in the footsteps of someone like you, it can be so hard to know and feel that you can do anything.

Mozumdar was flawed. His assimilation to American society internalized its racism. In order to make himself palatable in the eyes of white Americans, Mozumdar adopted their slurs and biases to make himself seem more similar to how they thought and viewed the world around them. Mozumdar distanced himself from the other immigrants white Americans saw with contempt, without challenging their views. He put down others of his own kind to make himself seem better. And he was not the first or last immigrant in the United States to do such a thing. I grew up surrounded by examples of other brown people who made it a point to illustrate that they were more like mainstream, white Americans than any other type of American in our vicinity. Mozumdar was the type of complicated figure the twelve-year-old me would like to have read about in *A History of US*. His story speaks to the complications so many immigrants in the United States face when trying to find where they fit in America's racial and social hierarchies. These experiences deeply shape the ways immigrants think of how they become American citizens. Most importantly, if Mozumdar was missing from my history books, who else was missing?

This question was at the top of my mind when, ten years after Mr. Best's social studies class, it was time for the next stop on my

West Coast research trip. I had finally received an email from a librarian in Berkeley that the materials I had requested to view were ready. I flew to California, drove across the San Francisco–Oakland Bay Bridge, and arrived on the campus of the University of California, Berkeley.

Bancroft is a research library with one of the largest collections of primary source materials documenting the lives of early South Asian immigrants in the 1800s and 1900s. It began as the personal library of Hubert Howe Bancroft, who began his career as a bookseller and later became a publisher and historian. Bancroft made it his life's mission to build the largest and most complete collection of books and materials about the North American west, stretching from Canada, through the United States, and Mexico. Bancroft traveled across the country and Europe purchasing books for his collection. By 1900, his collection grew to around 45,000 books, which he kept in a fireproof building monitored by a team of assignments. As Bancroft's reputation grew, he began to acquire original documents donated by governments and families up and down the Pacific Coast. (One document that would gain notoriety was the diary entry of Patrick Breen, a frontiersman who was part of the Donner Party, a group of people who may have resorted to cannibalism when they got stranded in the middle of winter in the Sierra Nevada Mountains.) Where Bancroft could not acquire original versions of documents, he commissioned replicas to be made.

In 1905, Bancroft's collection was valued at $300,000 or almost $9 million today. Looking for a permanent home of what would become the largest collection of books about the people, countries, and physical nature of the Pacific Coast, Bancroft decided to sell the collection to the University of California, a fitting home. The collection sold for $55,000, or about $1.5 million today. Bancroft had two stipulations. First, the library had to in perpetuity bear his name. Second, the university had to commit to growing and expanding the core collection to remain the preeminent source of materials about the North American west. Over one hundred years later, both terms have been upheld.

To get to the library I had to walk through Berkeley's campus. The weather was sunny and warm, the smell of fresh-cut grass was in the air. Students sunbathed on the lawns that led to the library. I could hear music and people laughing around me. On this leg of my research trip, I was reminded of everything I loved about college: the immediate access to a lot of the world's knowledge and a relatively carefree time before adult responsibilities set in. It was one of the few moments where I could genuinely orient everything in my life toward learning.

The Bancroft Library is a large, white building that is much wider than it is tall. Its front facade bears three rows of tall, paned windows. It has no columns but still manages to feel like it contains a classical gravity associated with the White House or the Parthenon. The building looks stoic but inviting. When visitors enter, they are greeted by a round foyer lit by soft lighting and tiled in gold, white, and blue hues. The entire space feels both formidable and approachable.

Although the Bancroft Library is a library in name, it is unlike the public libraries most of us are familiar with. The Bancroft Library does not lend books. Unless certain conditions are met, the books cannot leave the building. Visitors cannot arrive to view or read books unannounced. In fact, most books and materials are kept out of sight and away from the public eye. Some of the books are so old that they're kept in climate-controlled storage facilities with no light that can fade or damage the pages.

When I arrived at the Bancroft Library, I had submitted a request to view collections on South Asian American history months in advance. A research librarian responded with the windows of time when the collections could be made available to me. On the specified time and date, I introduced myself to a security guard who checked to make sure I was not bringing in any contraband items. Items that count as contraband for research libraries can vary. The security guard checked to ensure I was not carrying any pens, ink, folders, binders, envelopes, boxes, cases that could contain papers, bags, purses, or professional cameras. I was allowed to bring my phone, only kept on silence mode, one notebook or five sheets of paper, and a pencil. Anything else I was carrying had to be stored in a locker outside the reading room.

Inside the reading room, I was met by one of the researchers who guided me to the materials I requested. She had stacked on a table over a dozen boxes that were a little too large to comfortably carry but each contained government and personal papers that told the stories of the thousands of South Asians living on the West Coast at the turn of the twentieth century. The biggest source of materials was local, state, and federal governments, but there were also numerous newspaper clippings and personal writings. I was allowed to work with only one box at a time, and I had eight hours to review everything before the library closed. I picked up my first box, carried it to my assigned research desk, and started.

It's actually a rookie mistake to do any research in a research library. It's tempting to take the time to read through every document, especially if they're hundreds of years old. It's a thrill to know you might be the first person to touch a particular document in a very, very long time. Unfortunately, there often isn't any time to do any reading. Luckily, I was prepared and had my camera phone with me. Fighting the temptation to sit down and just read, I diligently took out my phone and started to take photographs of every document that was in each of my boxes. As I took my photographs, I started to see the effects of Mozumdar's citizenship case.

Whether he realized it, Mozumdar's argument for citizenship in Judge Frank Rudkin's court was historic. Mozumdar established a legal precedent that brown-skinned South Asians were legally white. Whenever a South Asian immigrant petitioned for citizenship after 1913, a court used Mozumdar's case to certify that the South Asian was not only a free person but also a white person as required by the Naturalization Act of 1790.

In the years following 1913, Mozumdar purchased his acreage in San Bernardino and continued on with his lectures. There is little to no record of Mozumdar meeting other immigrants like him or knowing that the small influx of immigrants from British India were starting to create headlines as they immigrated to the United States and became citizens themselves.

South Asian immigrants who had become American citizens started to build a life for themselves by owning property and accumulating wealth. I discovered within this company so many diverse ways of living, which challenged assumptions I realized I had growing up that all immigrant life was largely similar. One group of people in the Berkeley collection had formed a hotbed of activism in San Francisco to convince the U.S. government to endorse colonial India's fight for freedom from the British Empire. Another group settled in Southern California, intermarried with people from Mexico or people of Mexican descent and formed a new type of American community that brought together their separate cultures and combined into something new. (If you are a fan of Indian and Mexican cuisines, you'll understand the possibilities that can happen if you combine the two. Years after completing research for this book, I returned to California and ate at a restaurant in Yuba County. It's been one of the best meals of my life.)

All the while, and unbeknownst to Mozumdar or anyone else, the U.S. government, through the Bureau of Naturalization and an alliance with Great Britain, watched. Judge Rudkin's court decision to classify South Asians as racially white was a decision that created uneasiness throughout the American judicial system and the rest of American government. There was little the government could legally do to reverse Rudkin's decision. Other courts had to honor Rudkin's decision in their own trials, and Rudkin received a promotion when President Warren Harding appointed him to the 9th Circuit Court of Appeals, a prestigious post he held until his death in 1931. The U.S. government, however, subverted the decision where it could. In one of four reports published in 1913 detailing the results of the 1910 census, the Census Bureau wrote, "Pure-blood Hindus belong ethnically to the Caucasian or white race and in several instances have been officially declared white by the United States courts in naturalization proceedings. In the United States, however, the popular conception of the term 'white' is doubtless largely determined by the fact that the whites in this country are almost exclusively Caucasians of European origin and in view of the fact that the Hindus, whether pure-blood or not, represent a civilization distinctly different from that of Europe, it was thought to classify them with non-white Asiatics."

According to the Census Bureau, the courts could declare "Hindus" to be white, but everybody knew, by popular definition, they were not. The Census Bureau made this statement in a footnote that appeared at the bottom of a table recording the racial makeup of the U.S. population. The statement hardly impacted the results of the Rudkin decision.

In order to reverse Rudkin, the U.S. government, through the Bureau of Naturalization, would have to appeal the citizenship petition of a South Asian immigrant in the U.S. Supreme Court. The question was, which immigrant would have a petition and personal history that could equip the government with enough ammunition to appeal?

It took me an entire day to photograph the entire collection at Berkeley's Bancroft Library. It would take me another month to read through personal diaries, old newspapers, and government records. Just as I was trying to learn about the lives of South Asian men and women living in the United States around 1913 to research this book, the U.S. government in 1913 began an effort of surveillance to find their key person to take South Asian citizenship to the Supreme Court.

Among the stories of hundreds of men and women I collected in my phone, one story of a tall, slim, and bearded young man named Bhagat Singh Thind stood out. Unlike Mozumdar, Thind's story seemed to be well known. Before I started my research trip, his story appeared on the first page of some my Google searches. His story was the only story I was really expecting to find in my own library research. I first found mention of Thind in Berkeley's own records of enrolled students and later discovered a photograph of him in a white turban and an American military uniform. Thind came to the United States as a student, and his story began exactly where I was in that moment, at Berkeley. The documents I obtained captured the lives of this man and his contemporaries during the 1900s, 1910s, 1920s, and beyond. Many of these documents contained evidence that the U.S. government used to choose who the right key person could be. And that key person became Thind. Mozumdar and other South Asians had no idea that their lives would turn upside down when Thind submitted his own petition for citizenship to the waiting U.S. government. But before all that could happen, Thind was just a twenty-one-year-old student walking on the same streets of Berkeley I had just walked.

That night, I left the Bancroft Library with what I brought with me and new photographs on my phone. There was something about discovering that I was part of a larger legacy of South Asian American college students that resonated with him. Walking through campus, past Sather Tower, I wondered what Berkeley might have been like in 1914, when Thind was a student. The building home to the Bancroft Library wasn't yet built, but the city of Berkeley had already become a forerunner for the arts and sciences, thanks to the university. I wondered if Thind felt as I had felt as a young college student, protected by a campus bubble and buoyed by nearly endless knowledge and nearly endless time, believing that anything was possible. Unfortunately, as I would find out when I got home and read more, the future was about to close in on Thind.

Seattle, July 4, 1913

As the United States celebrated its birthday and Mozumdar enjoyed his first few months as an American citizen, Bhagat Singh Thind arrived in Seattle aboard the *Minnesota* from Punjab, India by way of Manila. In government documents, Thind stated he was born in Punjab on October 3, 1892, just a few months shy of being twenty-one years old when he arrived. Thind was described by immigration clerks as roughly 165 pounds, six feet tall, with a dark complexion, dark brown hair, and brown eyes. He had no visibly distinctive marks on his body. We don't know exactly what he wore on the day of his arrival, but there exist photographs taken aboard the *Minnesota* when it docked in Seattle. Aboard the ship, these photos show young brown men who looked the same age as Thind. They wore clean, sharp three-piece suits with ties and their jackets properly buttoned all the way down the front. One man in a photograph wore a white pocket square. Nearly all the men photographed wore white turbans. Although we do not have photographs of Thind aboard the *Minnesota*, the color of Thind's skin did not matter. Legally, Thind was a white man.

Punjab is located in the northwestern corner of India, and when compared to the northwestern corner of the United States, Punjab and the Pacific Northwest could not have been more different. The Pacific Coast experienced more rain than Punjab. The vast evergreen forests that stretched from Northern California, Oregon, Washington State, and into Canada were in remarkable contrast to Punjab's flat stretches of wheat fields and farmland.

In Punjab, Thind was raised in a Sikh family. Sikhism is one of the major religions of South Asia and originated in the Punjab region in the fifteenth century. It quickly attracted converts from Hinduism and Islam with its belief that the material and spiritual worlds that defined humanity could and should coexist. He was taught philosophy and religion by community gurus and was raised to become a spiritual leader. He attended Khalsa College in Amritsar, and it was there, while reading the works of Ralph Waldo Emerson, Walt Whitman, and Henry David Thoreau, that Thind decided to move to America. After arriving in Seattle, Thind headed south and found work in Alderbrook, Oregon at the Hammond Lumber Company.

The Hammond Lumber Company was founded by an entrepreneur named Andrew Benoni Hammond who had made his fortune in the railroads. The Hammond Lumber Company was the largest employer in Alderbrook. Six hundred men went to work cutting trees, loading logs onto rails, and transporting them to lumber mills where they would be trimmed, sliced, and then packaged and sold as construction beams. By 1914, one in six of Hammond's employees were from India. These Indians were mostly from Punjab and mostly Sikh. One hundred of Hammond's Indian workers lived in a small shantytown outside of Alderbrook that locals came to call Hindoo Alley. Hindoo Alley is where Thind made his first home in the United States.

Hindoo Alley wasn't just home to the employees of Hammond but also the employees of several nearby lumber mills. Hindoo Alley was also home to workers who were Greek, Japanese, and Arab. Arab workers were often confused for Hindus by the white locals. Indeed, there were very few, if any, actual Hindus living in Alderbrook or the surrounding town of Astoria. Hindoo Alley was actually a misnomer. The overwhelming majority of people living in this area were from South Asia but were practicing Sikhs. It is estimated that between 1830 and 1930, almost 30 million people left modern-day India. Some of these men settled in other parts of the British Empire, such as Singapore, South Africa, and Australia. They left to escape a plague that, by 1907, was sweeping through northern India, spanning the lands between Calcutta in the east and Punjab in the west. They also left to escape increasing political unrest as the Indian independence movement began to gain traction. It would be anti–South Asian sentiment in South Africa and Australia that encouraged more immigration to North America.

This first wave of South Asian immigration, grossly understudied and underrepresented in today's history books, began over one hundred years before when most historians attribute to the beginnings of South Asian immigration to the United States—the 1960s. This immigrant group was diverse. It contained people who today would be Indian, Pakistani, or Bangladeshi. It contained people who practiced different religions: Hinduism, Sikhism, or Islam. And it contained religious teachers, intellectuals, students, farmers, laborers, and mill workers. Whereas students and people like Mozumdar were likely to live and travel in various parts of the country along the West and East Coasts, people who were laborers were most likely to live and work in the American West. Popular immigration routes at the time connected British colonies in Asia to British Canada, particularly British Columbia. But in 1908, immigration from South Asia was banned in British Canada. Of the 8,000 South Asian migrants living in British Columbia, it is estimated 7,000 migrated southward to the United States, concentrating in Washington State, Oregon, and California.

Local Oregon history is also quick to point out that Hindoo Alley wasn't just an alley but a set of communities that resided in the cities along Oregon's winding Columbia River that included Seaside, Astoria, John Day, Clatskanie, Rainier, Goble Saint Johns, Linnton, Bridal Veil, Hodd River, and The Dalles. Records from the 1910 census indicate that there were dozens of men, predominantly Sikhs, living in each of these cities. The largest concentration, of course, was in Astoria, home to Hindoo Alley. Motivated by the high demand for construction materials to help grow and build cities and towns across the American West, lumber mills in Astoria were flush with jobs. It is even believed that Andrew Hammond himself took a trip to India to recruit workers. For Hammond, there were too many trees and not enough men to cut them down. This later proved unnecessary.

Hindoo Alley had a central cookhouse that was shared by all residents. The men cooked Indian food, rolling chapattis with their bare hands because they lacked the proper utensils. Families and women were exceedingly rare in Hindoo Alley. There was one South Asian family, and quite possibly the only South Asian family, in Hindoo Alley. They were the Dhillons. Bakhshish Singh Dhillon lived with his wife, Rattan Kaur, and their children, Kartar, Budh, Kapur, and Karm. According to the recollections of local residents, the two Indian boys named Kapur and Budh were of school-going age and attended a nearby public school in Astoria. There was little to no tension between the men of Hindoo Alley and the local residents of Alderbrook. They shared common interests, such as wrestling, and had mutual respect in each other's work. A local resident recalls that immigrant workers never agreed to lower wages to secure work at the cost of others, despite this being a prevalent stereotype of immigrant workers. The men worked ten-hour shifts, five days a week, and made two dollars a day. They paid one dollar a month in rent for single bunkhouses that could accommodate four beds. Photographs of Hammond Lumber Mill show these houses tightly packed together, so close that their roofs touched, and built within walking distance to where lumber was loaded and sent off in ships on the Columbia River.

Other photographs show mill workers white and brown (remember, legally they're all white), sitting shoulder to shoulder on stacks of lumber so large you can with little imagination smell the sharp pine. These men dressed in loose slacks and overalls, vests and jackets that were not tailored or ironed. Some of the brown men wore turbans and kept their beards long. Others were shaven and wore Western hats with brims to keep out the sun. Although the lives of these men likely revolved around the mills where they worked and lived, evidence shows that they were still politically active and large enough in numbers to organize. On May 30, 1913, an advertisement appeared in the *Astoria Budget*, a local publication, announcing that a man named Munssi Ram, who was secretary of an organization called the Hindu Association of Astoria, Oregon, was inviting readers to a talk at a local building called the Finnish Socialist Hall given by a professor from Stanford University named Har Dyal. Dyal was a "noted philosopher and revolutionist in India" and was planning to give a "lecture on India for the American residents of India."

Thind worked and saved his money for two purposes. Unlike Mozumdar, Thind did not receive an allowance from his family back home. Instead, Thind sent money to his father to help the family's farming and to support his brothers. Letters between Thind and his father reveal that Thind was concerned over family debts and was eager for his father to use the money Thind made to purchase more land and to get his brothers married. Thind's second purpose was to save for college. Students of South Asian origin in colleges across the country were rare but not unheard of. They were usually the children of India's elite. The son of the 1913 Nobel Prize winner poet Rabindranath Tagore was a student at the University of Illinois Urbana. The prince and son of the maharaja of Barooda was a student at Harvard University. And there exist records of South Asian students at Columbia University and colleges in Nebraska and Iowa.

For Thind, Berkeley was the best fit. California's climate was quite similar to what Thind would have grown up in. Tuition was inexpensive. Tuition at Berkeley in 1914 cost $15 a year and an average of \$250 a year for living expenses. Thind worked each summer at the Hammond Lumber Mill, and used that money to pay for Berkeley courses.

Berkeley in 1914 might have seemed like a different world compared to Hindoo Alley. The city of Berkeley had adopted many modern conveniences thanks to research and financial backing from the university. Thind would have enjoyed streets lit by electric lights. He might have traveled by electric-powered streetcars. He could have made calls (albeit only local calls) using the city's new telephone system. And if the city of Berkeley seemed to be from the future, Berkeley's university campus was like a different planet.

Berkeley's professors and faculty conducted research at the forefront of their fields, and their progressive ways were adopted across campus. When research suggested that alcohol had negative impacts on the human body, the university banned alcohol on campus (likely to the chagrin of its young study body) almost fifty years before Prohibition gained a hold of the national consciousness. Berkeley admitted and taught women and men equally, almost a century before the nation's top universities would become coeducational. Indeed, women were pillars in Berkeley's community. Phoebe Hearst (the mother of William Hearst, who founded Hearst Magazines) served on Berkeley's board of regents and donated a substantial amount of money to build and expand Berkeley's campus. By the time Thind arrived on campus, Berkeley had educated and graduated the likes of Rube Goldberg (famed engineer and Pulitzer Prize–winning cartoonist), Annie Alexander (founder of the Museum of Vertebrate Zoology and the Museum of Paleontology), Julia Morgan (the first woman to become a licensed architect in California), and May Cheney (a founder of modern standardized teaching).

Thind stepped into this world in 1914 and took classes in psychology and philosophy. He developed a keen interest in the law. But he soon discovered that Berkeley was not just at the frontier of American life; Berkeley was also a center point for the future of life in India.

Student life at Berkeley for South Asians was hard. Berkeley's social life across campus was dictated by Greek fraternities, which did not admit foreign students. South Asian students at Berkeley tended to live and study together. They received the support of faculty who studied South Asian culture and language, such as the Sanskritist Arthur Ryder (Berkeley was one of the first universities to devote research and academics to the field of linguistics). But South Asian students were largely reliant on themselves and each other. One student named Sarangadhar Das devoted much of his time to organizing South Asian student life.

Das ensured that students like Thind had a support system at Berkeley. Living expenses could be offset by the generosity of South Asian benefactors. One society called the Pacific Coast Khalsa Diwan purchased a hostel near campus and offered students free housing. One potato farmer named Jwala Singh, who had accumulated some wealth in California, established a scholarship for students wishing to leave India and travel to the United States for better education. (One advertisement, circulated in magazines in Calcutta, advised prospective students on what to pack for life in America: "soap, shaving brush, a pair of pump shoes, line athletic summer underwear, colored or striped shirts (not plain or plaited, half dozen), a pair of Paris garters, one black serge suit, an Indian-made artistic scarf pin, a few dhotis, and two collar studs"). The Hindustan Association of America was founded by a student named Tarakhnath Das and had chapters across many college campuses in America, including Berkeley. It printed a journal called the *Hindustanee Student*, which provided additional guidance and community for students like Thind.

Interestingly, many of the South Asian students at Berkeley intended to return home after the completion of their studies. They seemed to have one of two goals: they either wanted to return home to fight for India's independence movement (taking with them what they had learned about American civics and government), or they wanted to return home to secure a high-paying and well-respected career in the Indian colonial government (taking with them a Western education taught by an esteemed ally of the British Empire).

One student named Darisi Chenchiah, from modern-day India, arrived on Berkeley's campus two years before Thind and described the student body and all of its aspirations in writing that would later be preserved by the Berkeley Library as part of campus history. "There were about thirty Indian students in the University of California, Berkeley at that time, comprising mostly Punjabees [sic] and Bengalees [sic]. . . . The Punjabee students believed in the overthrow of the British Rule in India by armed revolt. . . . The Non-Punjabee students wanted to devote their attention to studies only, pass the examinations, return to India with a loyal political record and enter Government service. . . . At the same time, they wanted to serve the cause of freedom if they could."

Any person, student or faculty, on Berkeley's campus who supported Indian independence was the subject of British surveillance. The British were aided by the United States who let their ally conduct operations to monitor the actions of immigrants and citizens on American soil. Although there were many people who sympathized with Indian independence within the United States, American policy toward India, and South Asia, was predicated by its alliance with Great Britain.

Surveillance did not stop Berkeley students from organizing. The Stanford professor Har Dyal had arrived on campus and was organizing Indian students out of a local Berkeley student hostel. He told students like Thind that although they were in school to prepare for careers, they all had a higher calling. "Prepare yourselves to become great patriots and wonderful warriors. Great suffering and sacrifice are required of you. You may have to die in this revolutionary cause," he told the young students. "Anybody can be a collector, or an engineer, or a barrister, or a doctor. What Indian [sic] needs today is warriors of freedom. Better death in that noble cause than living as slaves of the British Empire."

With these words, Har Dyal formed the Ghadar Party. Dyal envisioned an organization, based in Berkeley, that would train freedom fighters to be sent back to India and mobilize support and funding for Indian independence in the United States. Students at Berkeley and other campuses signed up. Thind signed up as well and became a founding member of the Ghadar Party. But unlike his fellow Ghadars, Thind had a lot more to lose. Whereas everyone else intended to go back home to fight for freedom, Thind wanted to stay in the United States and become a lawyer. And in the United States in 1915, only American citizens could practice law; Thind would have to naturalize. But first, he had to fight with the Ghadars.

9

Freedom Fighters

Berkeley, California, 1912

Twenty-eight-year-old Har Dayal was a resident of Berkeley who had lived in New Delhi, Oxford, Paris, and Martinique. The roundness of Dayal's face was matched by a pair of small, perfectly round eyeglasses that framed his beady eyes. He wore his hair parted neatly to one side, kept a neat moustache that was trimmed to fit the center of his face, and dressed in suits just as neat and as fitted. Dayal was considered an intellectual. He taught philosophy at Stanford University. He was an avid reader of Karl Marx and Buddhism and befriended German communists and Punjabi farmers. Despite being well traveled and having friends from different walks of life, Dayal always intended to return to India and ignite an independence movement that would free his country from British colonial rule.

In Berkeley, Dayal found a community of Indians who thought like him and, more importantly, had the funds to train freedom fighters in India and win support for their cause on the international stage. Between 1912 and 1913, this community organized across California, Oregon, and Washington State and founded the Ghadar Party.

"Ghadar" in Punjabi means "revolution." Dayal began his part in the revolution by purchasing a printing press and setting up a headquarters in San Francisco at 436 Hill Street. He recruited students from the Berkeley campus to publish articles advocating for

Indian independence. They published these articles in the party's official newspaper, the *Hindustan Ghadar.*

The *Hindustan Ghadar* was printed for the first time in 1913 in Punjabi and Urdu, languages that were commonly understood by the Indian farmers who lived in California, Oregon, and Washington State. The *Hindustan Ghadar* argued for why India needed its freedom from Great Britain. The newspaper solicited donations, which farmers eagerly gave, and served to provide updates across the Pacific Ocean between India and the United States.

To further distribute the newspaper and empower the Ghadar movement, Dayal tasked young men like Bhagat Singh Thind who traveled to farms owned by Indians to circulate newsletters, collect funds, and give rousing nationalistic speeches. Thind is known to have returned to Hindoo Alley and Astoria, Oregon for such activities as late as 1916.

Because Great Britain was an ally of the United States, a publication like the *Hindustan Ghadar* and its parent organization, the Ghadar Party, were considered subversive activities by the U.S. government. People like Dayal who were actively trying to recruit people for acts against an American ally made the situation worse. As Dayal coordinated the Ghadars, the U.S. Immigration Service recruited William Charles Hopkinson to track him down.

Technically, Hopkinson was an Indian. He was born in New Delhi in 1880 and was raised in a British family. His father was a sergeant instructor in Allahabad. Hopkinson spoke Hindi fluently and worked as a police officer in Calcutta. Sometime between 1907 and 1908, India's colonial government sent Hopkinson to Canada as an intelligence officer on behalf of the Criminal Intelligence Department in India. It was his job to uncover seditionist activities against the British Empire in North America.

Because Hopkinson spoke Hindi fluently, he was able to infiltrate Ghadar activities across Canada, Washington State, Oregon, and California better than other officers. Hopkinson was able to collect the most intelligence on the Ghadar Party, such as a list of named men who were part of the Ghadar organization. At the top of that list was Har Dayal. On Hopkinson's evidence, the United States moved to arrest Dayal in 1914.

Dayal's stint in jail was short-lived because he was released on bail. Since Dayal had been identified by the British, he could no longer serve as the leader of the Ghadar Party. Before Dayal fled to Switzerland, he appointed a man named Ram Chandra to lead the Ghadars in the United States.

Chandra and Dayal had met on Berkeley's campus. Chandra's ability to work with the Germans made him an ideal president of the Ghadar Party. As soon as he assumed the presidency, Chandra began sending his freedom fighters to India.

On August 4, 1914, Great Britain declared war on Germany and began World War I. That same day, Chandra prepared for his own war. Standing in front of the S.S. *Korea*, an American steamship bound for India, Chandra looked at the dozens of men before him, all of whom were exiled or self-exiled nationalists from Punjab united in their desire to expel the British from their homeland. The men stood ready alongside the San Francisco dock. With Great Britain threatened by German aggression, it was the perfect time to attack. Chandra had secured funds from German agents working in the United States to fund a mission to India to spur rebellion.

The men strained to hear Chandra over the steady rumble coming out of the steamship's two large smokestacks. "Warriors," Chandra began, "if you start to mutiny now you will put an end to the British government. Because on the one side Germany will attack her, and on the other side you will attack her." Chandra stood on the dock as the men boarded the S.S. *Korea*. He remained behind and coordinated India's Independence movement in the United States.

In his first year as president of the Ghadar Party, Chandra was routinely followed by British and American intelligence agents. They discovered that Chandra was in regular talks with a German agent named Mueller. Mueller and another German agent named Brincken frequently visited Ghadar Party headquarters to pick up pamphlets printed by the Ghadars. The pamphlets were intended to raise awareness of the Indians in the United States of a potential alliance with the Germans against a shared enemy, Great Britain. British agents discovered a box of pamphlets after searching Brincken's car in 1914 that read "Don't fight with the Germans, because they are our friends" in Hindi.

The Germans agreed that if Chandra could organize a group of Indian nationals to return to India to fight, they would fund arms for the Indians and supply a ship, the *Maverick*, to make the voyage.

Under Chandra, and with guidance from Dayal abroad, the Ghadar Party grew from a North American organization that received funds from local farmers to an international organization that received funds directly from the German government.

Between 1914 and 1916, an alliance was formed between the anti-British Indian nationals in San Francisco and the German agents operating along the West Coast. According to letters obtained by American agents between a Ghadar Party secretary named C. K. Chakravarti and a contact in Berlin, the Ghadar Party received $1,000 each month from the German consulate in San Francisco. In today's currency, that monthly sum amounts to $26,000. Chandra maintained four accounts for the Ghadar Party at the Mission Bank. Bank statements found by American agents at a Ghadar Party satellite office on nearby Valencia Street revealed that the money from the four accounts were used by the Ghadar Party to pay for utility bills, printing costs, and staff salaries.

In that same office on Valencia Street, American agents also found evidence of a secret, fifth account that was held in the name of Ram Chandra, not the Ghadar Party. This account contained $13,000 (today's equivalent of $334,000) wired from the German consulate. The account was in existence for two years and a secret to everyone except Ram Chandra. The secret account would divide the Ghadar Party into two competing factions.

San Francisco, 2016

On a residential block in the Laurel Heights neighborhood of San Francisco is a white, two-story complex tucked between a private home and an apartment building. Located at 5 Wood Street, this complex is home to the only memorial in North America to the Indian independence movement born in San Francisco in the 1900s, the Ghadar Party. Outside of North America, there is a sister memorial in Punjab, India. To an onlooker, 5 Wood Street looks like any other home built into the edge of a hill. But a discreet sign hung over the door reads, in Hindi and with an English translation, "Ghadar Memorial."

The Ghadar Memorial is one of San Francisco's lesser-known historical sites. My Uber driver hadn't heard of it when I told him where I was going. When Google Maps told us that we'd arrived at my destination, he took one look at the building and turned back to me. "Are you sure this is it?" The Ghadar Memorial isn't billed as a tourist destination. Getting out of the car, I decided to stand across the street and just look at the building to see if I felt any sort of affinity or connection. I did not. Of course, 5 Wood Street is not the actual site of the original Ghadar Party headquarters. That would be the original building at 436 Hill Street, which had since been torn down.

The Ghadar Memorial is owned and maintained by the Indian government. To visit, I had to first make an appointment with the Indian consulate. Although I had my appointment, on the day of my visit there was nobody inside to let me in. I knocked on the door and tried to walk around the building but didn't find anyone. I called the consulate multiple times until a representative put me on hold. It was clear that I had hit a bump in my research. I wasn't sure what to do. I considered knocking on the doors of neighbors to ask if they could tell me anything about the Ghadar Memorial or to help me get inside, but I was too shy. I thought about leaving and coming back another day, but I was already so close. I had flown to San Francisco with the sole purpose to visit this memorial. I decided to stay and wait around. I sat on the curb across the street and stared at the building willing someone to come out, with my phone pressed to the side of my face, a busy signal buzzing in my ear.

What's interesting, and frustrating, about research is that it can very easily exceed or betray expectations. I was expecting to visit the Ghadar Memorial and discover details about Bhagat Singh Thind that would bring him to life. I wanted to understand his motivations and walk in his shoes. Instead, I was stuck outside playing phone tag with the Indian government. The other funny thing was despite being Indian, I never once expected at any point in my research journey would I have to actually encounter or deal with a person or an institution from India.

I always thought, based on the experience of my own parents, that to immigrate to the United States and become an American inevitably meant leaving a home country behind. For the immigrants I was discovering in my research, they left behind India and chose to build a new life in the United States. From my point of view as someone born in the United States and automatically made a citizen with no effort, raised to believe in American exceptionalism, and living in a time where the United States is a major global superpower, an immigrant's decision to choose America is a no-brainer.

What made the Ghadars so interesting to me, I realized as I redialed the Indian consulate, was that despite choosing to come to the United States where they were able to accrue wealth not imaginable back home by taking advantage of opportunities in employment and education that were not available under colonial rule, Har Dayal and Ram Chandra were still so passionate about what was right for India. Perhaps on some level the feelings that motivated Dayal and Chandra were the same feelings that motivated my own mom and dad when they donated money back home or stayed up to date on the latest news from India.

I suppose no immigrant to the United States truly leaves behind their home country. But the immigrant experience has an inherent tension intertwined with the desire to leave the native home, the desire to adopt a new country, and the desire to remain connected to their original home. Balancing all three is difficult, and the United States, in any part of its history and for any group of people, has only made it harder.

Immigrants are primed to shed as much of their past as possible. The more "American" an immigrant can seem, the easier their assimilation experience and the more likely they are to be American. Ram Chandra and Bhagat Singh Thind were both immigrants who made very different choices between their home country and their adopted country. Chandra chose India. Thind chose the United States.

The Ghadar Memorial simultaneously shrinks into the streetscape and stands out with its Hindi signage. It is an important chapter in the story of how the historical South Asian community in the United States became South Asian Americans. There is a lot at stake for immigrants choosing their new country, and this was especially true of Indians choosing between an India that needed its countrymen in the fight for freedom and a United States that offered a future with more opportunities than anywhere else. Each choice brings with it risk and uncertainty. And at the end of the day, a person can only do what seems to be the right choice at the time for them.

It's hard for me to judge the actions of Chandra and Thind over a hundred years later. Chandra might have embezzled funds from an organization that was fighting for his country. Thind was eschewing his home country for the United States. Perhaps they were both only acting as individuals and not as citizens.

Up until now, all of my research about Mozumdar, Thind, and all these other characters was through the lens of them becoming, or not becoming, American. But as I sat across a building owned by India on a street in an American city, I was starting to feel even more confused about why countries had such an impact on our identities.

San Francisco, 1916

The Ghadar Party in 1916 had a sophisticated organizational structure. While most members like Bhagat Singh Thind traveled and gave speeches to fundraise and spread the cause, a smaller group of men comprised the inner circle of Ghadar Party leadership. This group included three men named Bhagwan Singh, Santokh Singh, and Ram Singh. (They were not related; Singh is a very common last name in Punjab, like Smith in America.) And all three men were suspicious of the secret account held in Ram Chandra's name.

On November 24, 1916, Bhagwan Singh wrote in his diary that he had asked Chandra to release all of the Ghadar Party's financial documents. Chandra refused. On December 8, 1916, Bhagwan wrote again that he asked Chandra to release their financials but this time in the presence of more Ghadar Party members like Santokh and Ram. Bhagwan added that a "good deal of discussion also took place about the accounts which Ram Chandra did not wish to render." Chandra turned over financial records to Bhagwan weeks later on January 4, 1917. In his diary, Bhagwan wrote that he discussed Chandra's records with Santokh and Ram later that week. On January 8, the three men visited the Mission Bank for themselves and discovered Chandra's secret account. They returned the next day and removed Chandra's name from the other four Ghadar Party accounts and replaced him with an Indian Muslim man named Ali Muhammad.

That month, the Ghadar Party split into two factions. The first, led by Bhagwan, alleged that Chandra had rerouted German money meant for the Ghadar Party to his own personal account and was likely an agent working for the British. The second, led by Chandra, alleged that Bhagwan, Santokh, and Ram were all colluding to betray both the Indians and the Germans. Chandra and his followers relocated their headquarters to 5 Wood Street. British and American agents added the house to a list of Ghadar-associated properties under surveillance. On August 4, 1917, three years after Chandra sent the first band of Ghadars to India, Chandra along with Bhagwan, Santokh, and Ram were all indicted for treason. By attempting to incite rebellion against an American ally on American soil, the Ghadar Party had violated American neutrality laws.

The threat of legal action made Bhagwan consider reconciliation between his faction and Ram Chandra. He wrote in his diary in April 1918 that before the men were scheduled to appear in court on April 16, they ought to come to an agreement to fight the charges of treason with a unified front. It is not clear if Bhagwan ever actually articulated his ideas of reconciliation to anyone. On April 4, 1918, Ram Singh walked into a pawnshop on San Francisco's Kearney Street and purchased a revolver from the shop's owner, William Schmalz.

Almost three months later, Bhagat Singh Thind began on a path different from his fellow Ghadar Party members. Although Thind was never part of the Ghadar Party group that was arrested, the U.S. government did place his name on a list of known extremists from India on the grounds that he had associated with people who conspired with Germany. The United States was not involved in World War I, and nationalism, coupled with a distrust of foreigners, was high. But despite the xenophobia and the anti-Indian sentiment Thind experienced at this time, he enlisted in the U.S. Army to become one of the first men of Indian origin to serve and one of the first Sikhs.

Thind was stationed at Fort Lewis, a newly built army training facility located in the woods of Washington State. A practicing Sikh, Thind fashioned a turban that complemented his military uniform. He can be seen standing out in every group photo of his battalion wearing his turban and a long, black beard in a sea of men with short hair and clean-shaven faces.

The Ghadar trial began on April 16, 1918 with Annette Abbott Adams, the United States' first female federal prosecutor, making opening arguments against thirty-two American, German, and Indian defendants. "Germans had the gold, the Hindus the greed," she told the San Francisco court. "Hordes of German agents swarmed to America and found willing conspirators in the Hindus." The prosecution's case spanned for days. More than a week later, on Wednesday, April 24, 1918, the attorneys for the United States still had not exhausted their list of witnesses and exhibits they intended to present to the court.

That Wednesday, at 2:00 p.m., Judge William C. Van Fleet declared a recess for the afternoon. Ram Chandra, who had been sitting in a box with other defendants, rose after Van Fleet left the courtroom and walked toward his lawyer, George H. McGowan. A spectator named J. E. Boyden, sitting behind the defendants' lawyers, saw Ram Singh, wearing a black turban, close the distance between him and Chandra. He appeared to fall forward and pressed a black object into Chandra's side. Boyden later wrote that he heard a sharp pop right before Chandra fell to the ground. "To me the report sounded like the peculiar plunk made when a boy naps a pin against a sheet of paper from a rubber band," Boyden wrote. "As the first bullet tore through Chandra's left side . . . Chandra suddenly shuttered and turned away. With his head lowered and his body waving, Ram Singh pulled the trigger three times more."

Chandra's body fell into the witness stand. Ram tried to get another shot but was seized by a man Boyden identified as Stanley Moore. Moore tried to wrestle the gun from Ram's hand when a U.S. marshal named James Holohan aimed his gun over the heads of attorneys, court officers, and onlookers and fired a single shot at Ram. Ram died instantly. "The bullet spun him as if he were a wax figure on a pedestal," Boyden wrote. "Then he sank in a heap, rolled over on his face and with a heave of his shoulders, died."

Annette Abbott Adams, who had crawled under Judge Van Fleet's desk, pointed at Chandra's body slumped over the witness stand. "He's still alive!" Boyden watched as a woman he did not know knelt beside Chandra and pressed two fingers into the side of his neck, looking for a pulse. "A physician would be useless," Boyden wrote. "Almost at the same instant Chandra opened his eyes, stared unseeingly and ceased to breathe."

Upon hearing that a murder had taken place in his courtroom, Judge Van Fleet ordered Holohan take into custody every Indian present. Members of Bhagwan's Ghadar Party faction told Holohan they suspected Chandra had misused funds Ram donated to the Ghadar Party. Ram, they said, smuggled the gun into the courtroom with the help of Santokh. One witness named Sundar Singh Ghalil reported to have seen Santokh hand Ram the revolver earlier that day. Bhagwan, Ram, and Santokh would all be charged in the murder of Ram Chandra.

The bodies of Chandra and Ram were cremated two days later on April 26, 1918. Eleven friends attended Ram's funeral and scattered his ashes at sea. Chandra's funeral was more elaborate and attended by fifty mourners. An Indian priest named Swami Masiananda delivered Chandra's eulogy, saying that the Ghadar leader would return to earth in another form to complete his work.

A week after the murder, Judge Van Fleet found the Ghadar defendants guilty of treason, but he sentenced them to serve only twenty-two months in prison. Despite a request from the British government, the U.S. Department of Justice chose not to deport the Ghadars. They remained in the United States, publishing pro-Indian independence materials and debating in editorials whether Chandra had actually been a British spy the entire time.

Later that year, Thind completed his enlistment. He was never deployed to battle and was honorably discharged on December 16, 1918, a little more than one month after the completion of World War I. His character, discharge papers noted, was "excellent."

Thind renounced all allegiance to India as soon as he stepped inside Fort Lewis in 1917. But that did not prevent him from fighting for Indian independence. As he would years later explain to President Franklin Roosevelt in a letter requesting aid for the Indian independence movement dated December 5, 1939, Thind would consider himself a composite of two halves. "I have the rare honor and blessed privilege of being born in the Sikh community of the great Indian nation," he wrote, "and have the still greater privilege of being an American" Thind was at once both Indian and American.

For Thind, the desire to remain connected to his Indian community and the desire to be an American were not at odds. And yet for the Bureau of Naturalization, which had been unsuccessful in blocking Thind's first attempt at citizenship, Thind's Indian heritage and American citizenship were incompatible. Their sentiment was not unique to Thind.

Since Mozumdar's landmark case, the bureau watched uneasily as South Asians applied for and became U.S. citizens. It was the bureau's perspective that these people earned whiteness via a loophole in the law, and not because they were actually white. Their presence, citizenship, and integration into American society threatened what it meant to be white, to be an American, and to be a U.S. citizen. The bureau looked to the laborers of Hindoo Alley who were supplying the wood that built American cities. The bureau looked to the Ghadar Party, who appreciated and adopted American values and ideals to their own cause for freedom. The bureau looked to individuals like Ram Chandra who had accrued large amounts of wealth. And Chandra was not an anomaly. South Asians in this time had begun to own property, build businesses, and invest back into their local economies. With a personal wealth of over $600,000 in 1915, a businessman named Vaishno Das Bagai started his own import business and ran a grocery store on San Francisco's Filmore Street called Bagai's Bazaar. Men like Bagai spoke fluent English, enjoyed fine tailored clothing, and the finer luxuries America had to offer. The bureau even looked at men like Mozumdar, who were building followings of actual Americans growing more and more interested in a culture that was not American.

Finally, the bureau looked at Thind, an American war veteran and Indian immigrant who was now petitioning to become a naturalized citizen. In the eyes of the bureau, Thind was a young, dark man standing at the nexus of the threats South Asians posed to American whiteness. By the time Thind applied and won citizenship in a district court, there had been enough confusion within the American courts system and critical commentary within the American press that it was time to settle once and for all whether South Asians were white. Most importantly, it was time to settle what it meant to be white in America. The year was 1920 and the United States Bureau of Naturalization chose to appeal Thind's case and assert its challenge.

Bhagat Singh Thind, an American citizen, was summoned to Washington, DC. It was time for Thind to travel away from the West Coast and fight for his citizenship in his country's highest court, the Supreme Court of the United States.

10

Citizenship on Trial

Washington, DC, 2016

New York City and Washington, DC are connected via 230 miles
of the I-95 and separated by three states: New Jersey, Delaware,
and Maryland. The interstate is an easy highway to drive. It's flat,
wide, and after years of federally funded (and unfunded) construction, well paved. On a bright, winter Wednesday morning, I
made the drive in just under four hours. There was no traffic or
construction stopping my dance with the speed limit. After spend-
ing so much time on the West Coast, it was good to be home. The
landscape of the East Coast is quite different from the West Coast.
Airports, highway rest stops, towns, and industrial yards scatter
across rolling green hills, not undiscovered but spared from
centuries of development. I whizzed by cities founded before the
Declaration of Independence was signed and towns settled by
Americans who immigrated from Europe or sold from Africa
against their will.

Much of colonial and early history of the United States takes
place on the East Coast. The nation's first capitol was New York
City. George Washington took his oath of office on the balcony
of New York's City Hall, which at the time was a building on
modern-day Wall Street, down the road from Trinity Church.
Today, that site is now a national memorial maintained by the
National Park Service. Trinity Church, over 250 years later, still

stands down the road, albeit both buildings are now flanked by concrete and glass skyscrapers.

It was on this site that the Naturalization Act of 1790 was drafted and signed on March 26, 1790. The next year, in December 1791, the nation's makeshift capital moved to Philadelphia, Pennsylvania.

For ten years, Congress debated the seat of American power before the northern and southern states reached a compromise in 1800 on the longer term location of their capital on a piece of land one hundred miles inland from the Atlantic Ocean along the Potomac River, today's Washington, DC. The decision to limit American citizenship to only white people was made by American men who commuted to the nation's capital from the north, along a route I was retracing, and from the south. The north and the south were the dominating geographic narrative of the 1800s. There was no East Coast United States and no West Coast United States. There was just the north. And there was just the south. I thought about this as I drove across the Delaware state border and enter Maryland, and in doing so passed the Mason-Dixon Line.

The Mason-Dixon Line was named after two surveyors, Charles Mason and Jeremiah Dixon, who were tasked with defining a border that was in dispute between the colonies of Maryland and Pennsylvania (including modern-day Delaware) in 1768. Both men died before the phrase "Mason-Dixon Line" actually became popular in American culture when in 1820 it was used to describe the geographic boundary between American free states to the north, where slavery was outlawed and African Americans could live freely, and American slave states to the south.

I was taught the Mason-Dixon Line's significance in demarcating the cultural differences between the North and the South that were born of different ideas about the American economy and race. In school, the Mason-Dixon Line was immutable and stark. The dichotomy between North and South was as clear as black and white. The subtle irony of my crossing this line on my drive to DC was never lost on me, especially as my research trips grew more extensive.

It's easy to feel, if you are not white or Black, that your own struggles with race or identity are not seen. For many white Americans, to be a minority is to be Black because the racial conversation in the United States has for so long been dominated by white and Black narratives. As I enter DC and drive down the National Mall, I pass buildings named after only white men (Lincoln, Jefferson, Washington) who did great things but entirely dependent on contributions of minority communities who do not have the same monuments erected to them. It shouldn't be forgotten that the Capitol was built on the backs of Black slave labor.

Even the National Mall, designed to recall the democratic ideals and intellectual purity of rationality born out of ancient Athens with its classical, Grecian-inspired architecture, is entirely composed of buildings made out of white stone. (Of course, as some amateur art historians might already know, whiteness as an aesthetic motif for idealism or purity in ancient Greece is a Western myth. Grecian and Roman sculpture was full of color.) As I found parking on a side street within walking distance to the U.S. Capitol building, it was inescapably obvious. The U.S. capital was very, very white.

Nevertheless, there I was, a brown Indian American woman striding along a white walkway and up a set of white steps to a large white, stone building. I was met with a set of three, thick bronze doors that were wider than my arms were wide and so high they appeared to completely tower over me. The doors were heavy, and as I pushed the smooth, cool, bronze with the palm of my hand, I embarrassingly looked up for some clue as to how to open the door and found myself staring at an art deco sculpture of Brahma, the Hindu god of time and creator of the universe, carved into the door. He wore a long dhoti, draped across his right shoulder and down to his ankles. In his left hand, he held a scroll.

Brahma was not alone. Next to him was Sequoya, a mortal man from the Cherokee Nation who created the first writing system, in the form of a syllabary or syllable-based writing, for the Cherokee language. Together Brahma and Sequoya were joined by Thoth, the Egyptian god of writing, the mythical Cangjie, who invented Chinese characters, Ogma, the Irish god who invented Gaelic writing, Nabu, the Akkadian god of writing, Odin, the Norse god who created the runic alphabet, and Itzamna, the Mayan god of writing.

These were all figures who had a part in the origin story of writing. And here they were, enshrined on the door of one of the most prized buildings in our country's capital. This was the United States I knew, the United States that was born out of the progress and enlightenment of cultures and worlds much older than it, adopting the best of these past traditions to create a modern state that was uniquely positioned to realize the ideals these older civilizations only dreamed about. This was the United States that was open to the whole world and everybody in it. This United States valued diversity and recognized its importance. Diversity meant anything was possible and that the stories of Bhagat Singh Thind, Sequoya, and even George Washington could be combined into a single shared national identity.

A security guard disrupted my reverie.

"Those doors are closed to the public," he said. He nudged my elbow and walked me to a security checkpoint down the street. The checkpoint had a barricade that prevented traffic along the side of the building. An armed man stood watch in a small booth. "You'll need to present your card for clearance," the guard continued.

I was still reeling from what I'd seen on those large bronze doors, but suddenly I was also very nervous.

"Like my driver's license?" I asked.

"No," he responded. "Your library card."

The world's largest library stands between Independence Avenue and East Capitol Street, in direct line of sight to the U.S. Capitol. It was the idea of James Madison. Madison reasoned that in order for a group of elected officials, the senators and representatives who would descend onto the nation's capital, to properly legislate, they would need access to the most up-to-date information of the day. At the conclusion of the Revolutionary War, the federal government occupied buildings in Philadelphia and New York, temporary capitals until Congress could decide where to make the nation's permanent capital.

The problem was a tricky one. Although the United States was "united" in name, the states were divided on things such as whether there should be a national bank, the legality and ethics of slavery, and where the nation's capital should be. The factions were along geographic lines, the North and the South. Neither wanted the capital in the other's region. A compromise was made in which a plot of swampland that was not too far south and not too far north was chosen—Washington, DC. And so, this would be the site of Madison's library for members of Congress, conveniently located from them right across the street.

Behind the doors adorned with the different gods of writing from cultures around the world are over 170 million items that spoke of American thought, culture, history, and government. To this day, the Library of Congress adds almost 10,000 items to its collection a day. Some of its collections are quite esoteric. There's the smallest book in the world, a copy of *Old King Cole* smaller than the size of a period at the end of this sentence. There's also the first book allegedly printed in the United States, a hymn book called the *Bay Psalm Book*, published in 1640 in Cambridge, Massachusetts.

The Library of Congress is overseen by the librarian of Congress, a federal position appointed by the president. It is the duty of the librarian of Congress to oversee the library's enormous collection, a staff of librarians who work across three buildings named after James Madison, John Adams, and Thomas Jefferson (who donated his own personal collection of books to the library). It is also the librarian's responsibility, interestingly enough, to appoint the United States Poet Laureate, a federal position unknown to most Americans but given the hefty responsibility of raising the national consciousness toward the powers of reading and writing over the course of a one-year term. (The poet laureate also receives a coveted office on the highest floor of the Library of Congress's Jefferson Building.)

By the time of my visit, there had been only thirteen librarians of Congress, all white men who had served lifetime appointments and lived in a pre-internet age. The thirteenth librarian of Congress, a man named James Hadley Billington appointed by President Ronald Reagan, courted some mild controversy when he expressed reticence at digitizing and making accessible online parts of the library's collection.

Later that year, in September 2016, Carla Hayden was appointed the fourteenth librarian of Congress, and she was the first female and first Black person to receive this honor. (Since her appointment, she has made it her mission to modernize and democratize to the public access to the library's vast amounts of primary source materials and knowledge. She has also appointed the first Native American poet laureate, Joy Harjo, and the first Chicano poet laureate, Juan Felipe Herrera.

By the time of my visit, however, access to our nation's largest and oldest library was hardly modern. First, I had to demonstrate an affiliation with a recognized academic research institution. Second, I had to apply for a library card that established my status as a verified reader. (Being issued my library card, complete with my photograph next to the Library of Congress insignia was one of the more thrilling moments of my research journey. The texture of the plastic card with its smooth edges in my hand brought me back to my first library card issued by the New York Public Library in Queens. How cool that I was now granted access to one of the largest libraries in the world.) When my application was approved, I was able to request the collections I wanted to view (like other research libraries, nothing can actually be borrowed or taken out of the library). And finally, I was given a date when I could make my visit.

After presenting my Library of Congress library card to security and leaving all my personal belongings in a locker (I was allowed to carry only my phone on airplane mode), I was free to walk around. It turns out the building with the bronze doors was the John Adams Building and served as an annex (although it was hardly the size of what I would consider an annex) to the main

Thomas Jefferson Building. The Jefferson Building is almost incomprehensible in scale, a sweeping Beaux-Arts monument complete with rotundas dizzying in size and gilded tributes to great men. Literally, as I would read online later, the set of statues on the second-floor entrance of the Jefferson Building are called the Great Men. These statues included the likenesses of Demosthenes, Ralph Waldo Emerson, Benjamin Franklin, Nathaniel Hawthorne, and Dante Alighieri. These were all indeed great men I had studied and admired in school, and I couldn't help but notice how similar in demographics the sculptures were to the other researchers and staff I encountered at the library.

My goal for my research in the Library of Congress was to view as many materials as I could about Bhagat Singh Thind. Thind had the distinction of accomplishing so many firsts on the national stage of the United States. He was the first Indian American to have a case heard in the U.S. Supreme Court and the first Indian American to serve in the U.S. military. Naturally, I thought he would have an obvious home in the Library of Congress. But there was no mention of Thind in the Library of Congress catalog, the guide to all materials in the library with references to where the materials were stored. It was almost as if he never existed.

History's biases are often reflected by who gets to tell the story. In the case of the Library of Congress's catalog, it ended up being reflected by how stories were organized. Although there were materials about Thind in the Library of Congress's collection, the items were not actually tagged to his name. Instead, they had been tagged by the more relevant (in the eyes of the tagger) people Thind encountered in his life.

One of these people was George Alexander Sutherland, an immigrant who almost one hundred years ago occupied an office right across the street in the U.S. Supreme Court where he served as an associate justice of the U.S. Supreme Court and wrote the deciding opinion in Thind's case. He was an immigrant from the right country (England), he was the right gender (male), and the right color (white). Indeed, the Library of Congress contained

4,500 items related to, or created by, Associate Justice Sutherland. These items were housed in eleven containers, each 4.4 linear feet long. I had to go through each item one by one, and by hand, to find anything that could tell me more about Thind's life. There were diary entries about the mundane (on January 9, 1884, he wrote a single line in pencil, "sick all day"), letters from presidents ("sincerely yours" Theodore Roosevelt hand-signed a letter to Sutherland in 1906), and overnight telegrams from family and friends congratulating him on career accomplishments.

Then finally, several boxes in and with my right wrist starting to ache from turning page after page of paper, I found Thind.

Washington, 1923

The U.S. Supreme Court in 1923 was comprised of nine justices of the Supreme Court, who were all white men. Former president William Taft served as chief justice. To this day, he is the only person in U.S. history to have held the roles of president and Supreme Court justice. Like his presidency, which was characterized by his lack of support for civil rights and racial equality (Taft chose to remove Black Americans appointed to positions in the federal government) and his support for immigration (Taft vetoed a bill that would have mandated all immigrants undergo a literacy test), the Taft court (periods of Supreme Court history are named after the chief justice who presided over that time) did little to advance civil rights for nonwhite American citizens.

On a cold Thursday in January, the U.S. Supreme Court assembled to decide whether U.S. Army veteran Bhagat Singh Thind should have been allowed to become a citizen of the United States.

On one side was the U.S. government, which took the position that the Bureau of Naturalization was correct to appeal Thind's citizenship on the grounds that he was not white. The government also contended that not only should Thind have never been given citizenship, but no person like Thind, an immigrant from Great Britain's Indian Empire should ever have been allowed to become an American citizen in the first place.

On the other side was Thind himself, represented by a local attorney from Oregon, and a man named Sakharam Ganesh Pandit. Pandit was an Indian immigrant from California, had himself become a citizen in 1914 after Mozumdar's citizenship case, and became an attorney. Pandit advertised his legal services in California newspapers, claiming to be "The Only Hindu Lawyer in the United States." Thind alleged that the precedent set by the lower court in Mozumdar's case ought to be upheld.

There is no written record of Thind speaking about his case. There is no known transcript of what his attorneys might have said during their allotted time for oral arguments. We also don't even know why the Bureau of Naturalization chose Thind's case to appeal to the Supreme Court over others. There is no record of the Bureau of Naturalization attempting to appeal the citizenship cases of other Indian Americans. And yet in this instance, the bureau decided to take its appeal one step further. Not only was it advocating for the repeal of a single man's citizenship, but it was also advocating for the revocation of citizenship from all Indian Americans living in the United States.

The Bureau of Naturalization justified this request to the Supreme Court by citing the Immigration Act of 1917, also called the Asiatic Barred Zone Act. This act banned all immigration from modern-day Asia including but not limited to China, India, Afghanistan, Burma, Thailand, and eastern Russia. The act was vetoed by President Woodrow Wilson but passed in Congress with a strong majority. There was too much anti-immigrant sentiment, coupled with a wave of nativism that was suspicious of foreigners who threatened to dilute American culture and society or put it on a trajectory for the worst. The act curbed the threat of Indians immigrating to the United States, but it did nothing to the people already living in the country. The Bureau of Naturalization watched as Indians became citizens well after the act became law. From the bureau's point of view, Indian American citizenship was not a sign of progress but a symptom of a system that was not adequately defending the intent of the founding fathers. Thind's petition for citizenship was the final straw.

It was against this backdrop the Supreme Court considered the case. There were nine judges, with former president William Taft serving as chief justice. Associate Justice George Sutherland had been appointed to the court only the year before in 1922. He had a long face with short hair parted neatly down the middle and a salt-and-pepper beard and moustache trimmed close to his face in a style common for that day. It was Sutherland's job to write the judicial opinion.

We don't have any indication that Sutherland ever met Thind. The men were born thirty years apart (Thind was younger) and came from opposite ends of the British Empire. Their lives converged in Washington, DC, but we have no evidence that Thind attended his Supreme Court hearing in person. What we do know is that there were innate similarities between the two men. Both men grew up with an interest in the law, both wrote in their later years a support for a person's individual freedoms when faced with the threat of an infringing government, and both men were immigrants.

George Alexander Sutherland was born in a small English town called Stony Stratford in 1862. Stony Stratford traces its history to Roman times and, according to history (or folklore, depending on who you ask), was where the phrase "cock-and-bull story" originated. Sutherland's father was Scottish, his mother was English, and both emigrated to the United States to follow the Church of Jesus Christ of Latter-day Saints. The followers of the Church of Jesus Christ of Latter-day Saints, or as we know them today as Mormons, had settled the frontier of modern-day Utah, Colorado, and Wyoming in what was then-called Utah Territory. Sutherland lived in Utah Territory throughout his childhood. He attended college at Brigham Young University and left for Michigan to study law at the University of Michigan. (Twenty-year-old Sutherland may not have enjoyed his time at Michigan, as he attended law school for only one year and wrote a particularly dour poem in his diary on Christmas Day in 1882.)

Sutherland did not complete law school. Nevertheless, he did receive admission to the Michigan Bar Association. This allowed him to start his own legal practice back in Utah Territory. He lived in Utah Territory for much of his adult career, seeing Utah transform into statehood when it officially joined the United States in 1892. Sutherland, who married a woman named Rosamond Lee and became a father to three children, helped found Utah's own state bar association.

Eight years after Utah's statehood, Sutherland was elected to represent Utah in the U.S. House of Representatives. Congressman Sutherland represented the entirety of Utah, which was not populated enough to warrant more than one congressional district.

After a short stint in the House of Representatives, Sutherland was elected to serve in the U.S. Senate in 1905. By now, Sutherland had established himself as a conservative and member of the Republican Party. It is important that readers do not project what conservatism would come to mean over one hundred years later. Sutherland was a conservative on many fiscal issues and was wary of government encroachment on individual freedoms. He was by today's standards also a liberal.

Alice Paul, a leading suffragist and feminist who was known nationwide in the early 1900s for her work to advance women's rights, considered Sutherland a friend. Paul dedicated her early career to organizing and galvanizing government and public support for the Nineteenth Amendment, which established the right for women to vote. Paul was the mind behind suffragist parades in Washington, the Nation Women's Party lobbying of Congress, near-constant protests outside the Wilson White House (which teetered back and forth from peacefulness), and the ultimate introduction of the Nineteenth Amendment to the U.S. House of Representatives and the U.S. Senate (done, in proxy, by Senator Sutherland).

Sutherland served in the Senate until he lost reelection in 1916. He remained in Washington, serving as the president of the American Bar Association. Sutherland's name was on the top of many lists for federal judicial positions. His private letters contain many correspondences from friends, colleagues, and admirers wishing him luck for various appointments and sending condolences for appointments that went to others.

Sutherland's time came on September 5, 1922, when President Warren G. Harding nominated him to the Supreme Court. Less than one year later, Sutherland was writing the unanimous opinion on Bhagat Singh Thind's case.

Sutherland first summarized the case into two questions: "Is a high-caste Hindu, of full Indian blood, born at Amritsar, Punjab, India, a white person?" and did the Asiatic Barred Zone Act "disqualify from naturalization as citizens those Hindus now barred by that act, who had lawfully entered the United States prior to the passage of said act?"

He deliberately made the scope of Thind's case to be larger than Thind himself. There is no mention of whether Thind satisfied the residency requirements (he did), or if he met the standards of good moral character (he did). The case didn't even ask if Thind specifically should have been a citizen. The case broadened to ask if people like Thind should become citizens.

Sutherland began his inquiry by quickly establishing that it was never the intent of the founding fathers to exclude groups of people from citizenship but to only state who could be included in American citizenship. He argues that if the founding fathers intended groups of people from Asia to be citizens, they wouldn't have omitted them but would have included them in their definition of acceptable groups, alongside white people.

Sutherland then began to unpack and dispute the idea that there was a scientific definition of whiteness and that this theory attributed any Caucasian person to be a white person. This was the theory that Mozumdar posited in his case, which Judge Frank Rudkin agreed with. According to Sutherland, "Caucasian" and "white" were not identical and it was a deliberate choice of words on the part of the founding fathers to use "white persons" in the Naturalization Act of 1790.

White persons, Sutherland wrote, "are words of common speech." As a result, whiteness had to be defined in a way that was widely understood by the common American. "The words of the statute are to be interpreted in accordance with the understanding of the common man from whose vocabulary they were taken," Sutherland wrote. To determine whether someone could be a citizen of the United States, it did not matter where that person was from or where their ancestors were from. All that mattered was whether that person, at the time of their application for citizenship, possessed the "requisite characteristics" they would have to have "in common" with other Americans.

What were these "requisite characteristics"? This is where Sutherland's language becomes vague, but he does demonstrate, by example, that even though two people could have a shared history, it does not mean they are the same. He wrote, "It may be true that the blond Scandinavian and the brown Hindu have a common ancestor in the dim reaches of antiquity, but the average man knows perfectly well that there are unmistakable and profound differences between them today."

Thind's attempt to establish an argument that he could be white was futile because all that mattered was whether another white American would look at him and consider him to be white as well. The science that Thind and Mozumdar attempted to cite was flawed and ultimately incorrect. But that didn't even matter. "We are unable to agree with the District Court, or with the other lower courts," Sutherland wrote, referencing Mozumdar's case, "in the conclusion that a native Hindu is eligible for naturalization."

"The words of familiar speech, which were used by the original framers of the law, were intended to include only the type of man whom they knew as white." This was by no means problematic nor at odds with immigration patterns. Sutherland noted that immigrants to the United States who came well after 1790 from places such as eastern, southern, and middle Europe "among them the Slavs and the dark-eyed, swarthy people of Alpine and Mediterranean stock" were all included in the American definition of whiteness. The intent behind the Naturalization Act of 1790 was to establish immigration from Europe and Europe only. It was not necessary to say this explicitly because a common American person (and Sutherland was clearly assuming this person could only be white; there was no consideration of African Americans, who were also citizens but not white) would be able to easily identify another white person and differentiate others who were not white.

"It is a matter of familiar observation and knowledge that the physical group characteristics of the Hindus render them readily distinguishable from the various groups of persons in this country commonly recognized as white." Sutherland does not place any value on the physical characteristics that separated Indian, and by extension Asian, immigrants from white immigrants, and by extension, white Americans. But he did note that these differences posed a practical problem that would prevent Indians, or Asians, from ever becoming American. He wrote, "The children of English, French, German, Italian, Scandinavian, and other European parentage, quickly merge into the mass of our population and lose the distinctive hallmarks of their European origin." This idea would be familiar to anyone who grew up learning in elementary school that the United States was a melting pot of cultures. Sutherland's next point would be familiar to any nonwhite immigrant child, like myself, who questioned their place in the American melting pot.

He went on to write, "On the other hand, it cannot be doubted that the children born in this country of Hindu parents would retain indefinitely the clear evidence of their ancestry. It is very far from our thought to suggest the slightest question of racial superiority or inferiority. What we suggest is merely racial difference, and it is of such character and extent that the great body of our people instinctively recognize it and reject the thought of assimilation."

In Sutherland's mind's eye, an American was white. A European was also white and by naturalization and assimilation could become American. But an Indian was brown and therefore, despite attempts at naturalization and assimilation, could never be American.

The answer to Sutherland's first question was simple. The only immigrants who could become Americans were European immigrants because only they were white. America was a white country.

To address his second question, Sutherland was also quite curt. "It is not likely that Congress would be willing to accept as citizens a class of persons whom it rejects as immigrants." Congress's ban on immigration from India was a clear sign. Thind and Mozumdar, and the people who looked like them were never meant to become American citizens.

What happened next was astonishing. When Sutherland declared that Thind could not be a citizen, he didn't just deny Thind's petition and set a precedent for all future immigration petitions from South Asians. He retroactively applied his decision to South Asian Americans who had already secured their decisions. This meant that people like Mozumdar who were already living in the United States as American citizens for years prior to the Thind case had to lose their citizenship.

Denaturalization is the process by which a country revokes citizenship from its citizens. In 1923, groups of people in the United States had been excluded from citizenship. Others had been given citizenship but not equal rights of a citizen. But no group of people had been given citizenship only for it to be taken away. Just to understand how extreme denaturalization in American history has been, I looked to the internet to find historic cases of denaturalization and found that denaturalization was typically reserved for people who committed war crimes, such as former Nazis who immigrated to the United States following World War II after managing to hide their actions during the war.

The process of denaturalization for South Asian Americans began.

11

The Aftermath

News broke of Associate Justice George Alexander Sutherland's decision on February 20, 1923. The American press and public officials across the country (and, it should be noted, that these individuals were all white men) were elated. The response to *United States v. Thind* was overwhelmingly positive. There are no records of any public figure taking Thind's side. Nobody questioned whether the court's ruling violated the civil rights of Thind, Mozumdar, or any of the other impacted Indian Americans. Based on the public's response, it was clear what the public thought about the whole affair. "Hindu" citizenship was an accident. The public believed that the United States should be free and open to only a certain type of immigrant: white immigrants. Only those who satisfied the white clause set by the Naturalization Act of 1790 could become Americans. Any other type of immigrant, of any shade of skin that was not white, was a threat to America's identity. Thind's case stopped the threat of nonwhite immigrant from coloring whiteness and the United States of America.

The *New York Times*, Associated Press, and newspapers up and down the West Coast carried the story. For most of the country, *United States v. Thind* was the end to a curious decade where brown immigrants who did not have the qualities required to become American citizens managed to become naturalized citizens. (Of course, their children born in the United States and therefore citizens by birth never had their citizenship impacted, but their citizenship was viewed as symptom of uncontrolled immigrant naturalization.) By going to the Supreme Court, the United States updated its body of immigration and naturalization law to maintain that whiteness was still a fundamental requirement of citizenship despite a more diverse influx of immigrants.

The U.S. solicitor general, fresh off winning the case for the United States went so far as to send a note to Justice Sutherland after the case. "My dear Justice," he began his letter, "I was amused by the following clipping, which I noted a few days ago, and thought you might be. I am yours faithfully." He attached a newspaper article to his letter. The letter ended in a succinct, tongue-in-cheek quip on the sheer complexity of Sutherland's decision. "Evidently a colored person is not white." For most of America, the decision was obvious. For Americans in the western half of the United States, the news was downright celebratory.

Newspaper editorial boards, particularly in California, lauded the news. "This decision of the United States Supreme Court, that Hindus are not eligible to American citizenship, is most welcome in California," declared the *Sacramento Bee*'s editorial board.

"This is surely an instance in which a court has decided on facts and not on inferences," wrote Fresno's *Morning Republican*. The *San Francisco Chronicle* weighed in, too, calling the decision "as important as the recent ruling holding Japanese ineligible to citizenship."

"We have already in this country all the race problems we can handle," the *Chronicle* continued. "We want no more and will not have them. The low-caste Hindus are degraded and the high castes made this country a center of agitation for their domestic feuds. . . . Their ways, their traditions, their thought, are not ours."

This was a common refrain found in multiple arguments that opposed Indians (and other Asian minority groups such as the Japanese) from becoming citizens. Only people who were white had a way of living that was compatible with American life. This argument even echoes Sutherland's judicial opinion. The child of a brown immigrant, born in the United States and therefore a citizen could never actually be an American. Because they were brown, they lacked the traits that came with whiteness that was required of all Americans. These traits are never explicitly described, and the argument in today's time holds little credibility. To use today's language, opposition to Indians' naturalization was founded on the basis of racist arguments.

Nevertheless, in the United States in the 1920s, the headlines gained momentum. A battalion of district attorneys across the country were dispatched with the task of revoking citizenship from Indian Americans who held it. The U.S. government repossessed land, property, and businesses owned by Indian American citizens. No citizen was compensated or given any leeway. Bhagat Singh Thind entered the U.S. Supreme Court a hopeful immigrant of the United States. He left the court a stateless person.

District attorneys tracked down Akhoy Kumar Mozumdar in Los Angeles in 1924. He had just started his own motion picture company with the goal of releasing a feature film called *Behind the Veil*. These plans were halted and his attention turned to saving his citizenship. Mozumdar attempted to appeal his case in the Los Angeles District Court and failed. A little over ten years after winning his case for citizenship in 1913, Mozumdar lost his citizenship on June 17, 1924.

All in all, district attorneys rescinded the citizenship of Indian American citizens wherever they could be found, concentrating largely in California. Sacramento, Sutter, Colusa, Glenn, and Los Angeles Counties all saw denaturalization cases. In San Francisco, district attorneys found Vaishno Das Bagai, the grocer and businessman who lived above his store with his wife and three sons, one of the few Indian American families to immigrate from India. He had become a citizen in 1921. Now Bagai was stateless.

Bagai lost his store, his home, and had no passport to even return to India. In 1928, Bagai rented a room in a hotel, kneeled into a hot oven, and waited until the gas replaced all the oxygen in his lungs. He left a suicide note addressed "to the world at large" that explained what drove him to death. It was published in the *San Francisco Examiner* on March 17.

In his suicide note, Bagai described in his own words what he thought was his American dream. "I have a good home, fine health, good family, nice and lovely wife, extra good children, few but best friends and a paying business," Bagai begins. "I came to America thinking, dreaming, and hoping to make this land my home. Sold my properties and brought more than twenty-five thousand dollars to this country, I established myself and tried my very best to give my children the best American education."

"In year 1921 the Federal court at San Francisco accepted me as a naturalized citizen of the United States and issued to my name the final certificate, giving therein the name and description of my wife and three sons. In last 12 or 13 years we all made ourselves as much Americanized as possible."

Bagai did try to become as American as possible. His brown skin was his ultimate barrier.

"But they now come to me and say, I am no longer an American citizen. They will not permit me to buy my home and, lo, they even shall not issue me a passport to go back to India. Now what am I? What have I made of myself and my children? We cannot exercise our rights, we cannot leave this country. Humility and insults, who is responsible for this?"

"I do not choose to live the life of an interned person: yes, I am in a free country and can move about where and when I wish inside the country. Is life worth living in a gilded cage? Obstacles this way, blockades that way, and the bridges burnt behind."

"Yes, you can call me coward in one respect, that I did not try to break the mountain with my naked head and fists."

Reading Bagai's suicide note is heartbreaking and captures in excruciating detail what happens when a government strips its citizens of their identity. Bagai simultaneously recognizes and wilts at the prospect of taking on America's mountain of whiteness. The pain is even more profound when the citizen is an immigrant, who deliberately and explicitly chooses their country in a way that non-naturalized citizens never have to.

By 1923, there were about 2,600 Indians living in the United States. The vast majority were men, with an estimated one hundred being women. All of these people would have felt the impact of Sutherland's decision. In California alone, "Hindus" owned 2,099 acres of land. On top of that, "Hindus" were farming on over 86,340 acres of land that they controlled under long-term land leases.

It's often the case that feelings of nativism, xenophobia, and distrust of people who don't look like us are motivated by economic fears. In California, people like Thind, Mozumdar, or Bagai did not own a majority of land or property. Nevertheless, the fact that they could purchase or work any land that could otherwise have gone to a white person was a problem. As the attorney general of California told reporters after the ruling, "The menacing spread of Hindus holding our lands will cease."

And it did cease. The United States reclaimed every last acre and piece of property that were owned by Indian Americans. The United States prohibited Indian Americans from leasing land or property. Unable to build a life for themselves in their adopted country and unable to return to their home country, Thind, Mozumdar, Bagai, and the nearly 2,600 people like them were forced into a stateless purgatory.

In 1923, there were no laws offering legal grounds for the federal government to revoke naturalization. The founding fathers spent a lot of time thinking about who could be an American citizen. At the heart of that question was who could be an American. As the United States opened more of its borders to immigration, Americans spent even more time defining American-ness against an onslaught of people who were seemingly not American.

It was surprising to me, as I read Sutherland's decision in the reading room of the James Madison building in the Library of Congress, that denaturalization could be ordered on such a large group of American citizens with little oversight or question. There was no debate over the ethics of denaturalization or if the Supreme Court of the United States had overreached its constitutional powers.

We have various examples of the United States denying citizenship to certain immigrants, of the United States giving groups of people citizenship but still treating them differently, and of remarkably rare cases of the United States stripping certain Americans of citizenship. But what happened to Indian Americans being stripped of citizenship because they never should have received it in the first place was a denaturalization process very few of us know about. The more popularly known cases of denaturalization (at least among American historians) in the United States happened primarily in the second half of the twentieth century. These cases were brought against Nazi war criminals who immigrated to the United States after World War II. These people, largely men, concealed their war crimes and Nazi pasts and assumed new lives as American citizens. When they were discovered and put to trial, the United States stripped them of their citizenship as part of their punishments.

I had always assumed that progress was linear and that society and government would naturally become more progressive as time went on. Up until this point in my research journey, I felt like I was observing the inevitable acceptance and inclusion of South Asians to the United States. But to read that the American government had so suddenly stripped these people, my people, of their rights felt personal. The whole point of my journey was to claim my home, the United States, by finding my place in its history. I was realizing that I'd have to make this claim despite some of its history.

To be clear, there is no guidance even in the U.S. Constitution on how to revoke citizenship for a group of people. The exception lies in cases where an individual has been charged with treason (but even then, the law around what is supposed to happen to a person stripped of their citizenship is fuzzy). For the first time in my research I felt worried. How tenuous was my status as an American citizen?

Washington, DC, 2017

One year passed after my visit to the Library of Congress. I was back in DC, but this trip had nothing to do with my research for this book. It was the Women's March on Washington, and I had driven in the night before with three of my best friends from college. We were angry, confused, and seeking catharsis we hoped to find with women who had descended onto Washington in response to the 2016 presidential election. Donald J. Trump had won the election with a campaign that was bitter and inflammatory. He attacked women's rights, civil rights, and immigrants. He fed to the dregs of American politics and identity the seemingly ever-present parts of the country that were convinced there was a conspiracy against an American way of life. He ran with the campaign slogan "Make America Great Again." One couldn't help but think, to what time was this person urging for America to return? A time when women weren't allowed to have credit cards or be allowed to vote? A time when Blacks and whites couldn't sit side by side in a movie theater or drink from the same water fountain? Or a time when immigrants who were not white could not become American?

Trump had just been inaugurated the day before. The next day, my friends and I woke up before dawn to take our spots in a sea of half a million demonstrators comprised of women and men from all ages and all walks of life. We were scheduled to march at noon but not before a long line of speeches from prominent people like actress Scarlett Johansson, singer Janelle Monáe, and New Jersey senator Cory Booker. But one speech, and not because it was the final speech that I remember it more vividly, came from then–California senator and now–madam vice-president of the United States Kamala Harris.

I hadn't heard of Kamala Harris before, so while she spoke, I did a quick search on Wikipedia. She occupied many positions in California government in which she was either the first woman or first woman of color. She was the daughter of immigrants. Her mother was from India. Her father was from Jamaica. And here she was, a South Asian Black American woman, giving a speech at one of the largest political events of the twenty-first century. As she spoke, her name began to trend on Twitter. Within seconds, people speculated that she would one day run for a higher office.

I stopped scrolling on my phone when a line from her speech caught my attention.

"Our country was founded on certain ideals. Ideals that we should all be treated equally," she started. "Founded on ideals where our immigrant communities represent the heart and soul of what it means to be an American."

The then-senator Harris, a daughter of an Indian immigrant and Jamaican immigrant, made her speech ninety-four years after Indian American citizens were denaturalized. Simply seeing her on stage reminded me that her presence, and even my presence, was evidence enough that not all had been lost in 1923.

Here we were, in Washington, DC, almost one hundred years later, in a sea of people so diverse and united. All of us were unquestionably American and unquestionably able to be American. Within this group I stood. And to this group Kamala Harris spoke. Clearly, the South Asian journey to American citizenship had not ended in 1923. Kamala Harris alone was enough proof that the idea of who an American citizen could be had been decoupled from racist objections to any person who was not white.

When the march ended, I took the DC Metro to a friend's house where I was staying the night and reflected on the day. Truthfully, the decision to come to Washington had not been easy. It was one year since I had visited the Library of Congress and one year since I had done any meaningful research. My journey had come to a standstill because I was having so much trouble reconciling my belief that I belonged in the United States with what I was learning about the American history of excluding South Asians from American citizenship. I no longer felt optimistic that the research I was doing would have any impact. I no longer believed that my sense of self could be rooted in American history. I could not be a self-respecting South Asian woman and a self-respecting American woman knowing the legacy that existed behind those two identities.

Back home in New York, I put away all my hard drives and notebooks. I ignored questions and requests for status updates from my editors and well-meaning friends. I instead put all my attention to my day job. None of these decisions felt good, but I justified it by telling myself that I had to focus on my adult responsibilities: earning a paycheck so I could pay the rent, pay the bills, and have some savings. Traveling the country to do research for a book about American identity and history was fun, but it was a distraction from the things that mattered. Every day, the news revealed a country that was so divided after the Obama presidency ended. Half the country seemed to be pining for a white America that never existed, and the other half pined for an America that we thought we had but quite possibly had never existed either. There was no point in reconciling these two halves; it was only exhausting.

But being at the Women's March and seeing Kamala Harris take the stage gave me hope. And as I thought more about the research I had done so far in Washington State, California, and Washington, DC, I started to think that even though I had ended my journey at a dark period of history, that history still continued.

Denaturalization didn't stop Thind or Mozumdar. Their paths to citizenship remained unpaved and longer than planned. But brick by brick, their paths were being resiliently laid by a new set of Indian Americans who would take up the cause. The South Asian American journey to citizenship had to span the tenure of the Naturalization Act of 1790 and all the events that would lead to its demise in 1952.

The American laws that institutionalized whiteness as a requirement for American identity would give way to the American laws that Kamala Harris would govern with. But it would take much longer for the impacts the racist naturalization requirements had on the mythology of American identity to recede. The Women's March on Washington, and Kamala Harris' speech that morning, was evidence enough. But the repeal of the Naturalization Act of 1790 was a major milestone in South Asian American civil rights and the transformation of American citizenship.

To continue on this journey to that important milestone, I had to get back on my research journey. In a research notebook, I scrawled a list of places and events I needed to track down. There was one place I had missed on my last trip to California. It was time to go back, to put myself in Berkeley in the years prior to World War II and in the lives of a family that could help me understand the next phase of South Asian American civil rights. We have a beautiful wedding to attend.

12

The Path to Acceptance

In 1935, Kala Bagai, in her home in San Francisco, received a proposal for marriage. The man was a family friend and someone Bagai knew well. But that he was asking someone like her was unusual. Bagai had a lot to consider before she said yes or no.

Twenty years earlier, Kala Bagai's face made headlines. In September 1915, the *San Francisco Call* ran a headline in all caps, NOSE DIAMOND LATEST FAD; ARRIVES HERE FROM INDIA. In normal styling, the *Call* printed a more explanatory caption: "Mrs. Kala Bagai, who has introduced the 'nose diamond' in San Francisco . . ." Below the caption, the paper included a large photograph of Kala. In the photo, Kala stares straight at the camera, her eyes are lined with kohl. She wore a light-colored sari that had a dark, embroidered border. Her hair was tied tightly behind her head. And as she stared straight ahead, she gave off the slightest hint of a Mona Lisa smile. "Old nose ring is out," the newspaper credits her saying. "See surgeon, then jeweler."

The article goes on to further quote Kala saying that nose diamonds were all the rage in India and that more traditional nose rings were becoming "passé." What follows is a succinct description for how exactly one gets a diamond nose ring. "Have your surgeon pierce your nose horizontally above the nostrils and just under the bridge; then order from your jeweler a little straight gold bar with a diamond set in one end, run it through the perforation, and—you're right up to the minute in fashion."

The fashion advice is compelling and a stark contrast to how newspapers, including the *San Francisco Call* previously covered Indian immigrants as a "Hindu problem." But perhaps the most compelling piece of information gleaned from the article isn't Kala's sense of style. Toward the end of the column, tucked away in the final paragraph, the *Call* includes the brief line, "She is the first Hindu woman to enter this city in ten years."

The exact veracity of this statement cannot be confirmed. Immigration or population records from the time period don't exist for minority groups at such a granular level. We don't actually know how many "Hindu" women lived in the United States, let alone San Francisco. What we do know is that it was exceedingly rare for girls or women to immigrate to the United States.

Families from what is today modern-day India who had the means (and open minds) were more likely to send their daughters abroad to England than to America. Young husband and wives from modern-day India were also more likely to immigrate to other parts of the British Empire, if they were to immigrate at all, to take advantage of jobs that could better support families. Immigrating to colonies in Africa or other parts of Asia simply provided more cultural proximity to the homeland than the United States. The immigrant most likely to come to the United States was young and male. Solo travel for a woman was out of the question.

There is evidence, of course, that some women immigrated to the United States from India. There is evidence of a mother living in Hindoo Alley with her husband and children. In her diary decades later, Kala would write about social events with other Indian women. But in 1915, and for much of her life, Kala was truly exceptional.

When she came to the United States, Kala was twenty-one years old. She had been married to her husband, Vaishno Das Bagai, since they were both nine years old. The marriage was happy, and they had three sons, Madan, Brij, and Ram. (It was also unusual to see young children make the journey to the United States. Ram was a baby when they arrived in San Francisco.)

The Bagais came to the United States with more means than most other immigrants, but their problems were similar. Kala could not speak, read, or write a word of English. Her husband encouraged her to learn the language by living with an American family, but she refused to live apart from her children. When the family attempted to move to Berkeley only to discover suspicious neighbors had changed the locks of the home they just bought to keep them out, it was her idea to live above their family store on Fillmore Street in San Francisco. A home above a store wasn't likely her idea of life in America, but this way, she could keep her children close and protected.

In India, the Bagais had servants, in-laws, and extended family to help with raising the children and doing household chores. None of these luxuries followed them to the United States. Kala learned to go to the grocery store and point at items she needed to buy, not sure of their English names. She found neighbors to help with childcare. And for reasons unknown to her, her husband taught her banking. She learned to invest money from their business (and later her husband's life insurance) into bonds and stocks. Kala never learned why her husband was so keen on taking her to their bank and introducing her to their American bankers, but she learned enough, and as she lived in California, she slowly became more and more American.

In family portraits, Kala traded her sari for Western-style dresses with short sleeves and a hemline that stopped at her ankle. She wore her hair short, parted to side, and in waves, a style popular through the 1920s. For all intents and purposes, life was challenging but good. Unbeknownst to Kala, things were becoming darker for her husband.

Other Indians were starting rumors. There were whispers that Vaishno Das was a spy for the British. He was paid for passing intelligence and his various businesses were just a front. Kala would remember neighbors being mean, which she just attributed to a type of jealousy that was inevitable in such a small community where the Bagais stuck out for more than just being Indian. The darkness became too much when Vaishno Das was stripped of his citizenship and left without a country to call his own.

There is no record of Kala directly speaking of her husband's death. We don't know if she had a suspicion, or if she knew he had rented a room for one night. We do not know where she was when she found out, or even how she found out about her husband's death. We don't know what she might have thought of the news reports and headlines that made all the gore that was meant to be private so public. We do know that when recounting the passing of her husband to her family, decades later, Kala would describe feeling lost and lonesome.

With no warning in 1928, Kala found herself in a foreign country where she could not speak the language, alone with no siblings or parents, and suddenly a single mother with three children.

Kala's first step was to learn English. She took classes in the evening at a local high school. Her second step was to ensure the family's finances were in order. She learned to diligently monitor her investments and developed a habit that continued for decades where she checked daily the highs, lows, and closing prices of stocks in her portfolio. (Kala was particularly bullish on Bethlehem Steel, noting in her diary when it closed one day on a soaring high.) Her third priority was to see that her children got married, and for that, a trip to India was needed in order to find suitable brides for her two older sons.

Years passed. In a family photograph taken in Chicago in 1933, Kala looks happy and self-assured. She wears a white dress with a delicate neckline shaped like a V. Her hair is short and in waves. On her neck is a string of pearls. On her face, she wears that same Mona Lisa smile as she stands surrounded by her three boys, all in suits, crisp white shirts, and ties, and all taller than her. They look like an American family. Even though the family was American in practice, they were not American citizens.

Kala's suitor came two years later. His name was Mahesh Chandra. He came to the United States in 1910 to study at Berkeley and Stanford, where he got his master's. He was a member of the Ghadar Party. He had no children of his own. They had known each other since Kala first arrived in the United States. Kala considered his proposal and offered one condition: If they were to be married, their families in India could never be told. (Even today, the stigma of second marriages for a woman are incredibly strong. Second marriages in India are exceedingly rare. In the 1930s, a thirty-five-year-old woman like Kala getting married for a second time was unheard of.) Mahesh agreed, and Kala accepted his proposal. The two were married and enjoyed a small party with close friends and what little family they had.

According to the 1930 census, there were 3,130 "Hindus" living in the United States, a modest increase from the 1920s but a surprising increase given that immigration from modern-day India was banned in 1917. Life for these 3,130 men, women, and children went on despite being stripped of their right to citizenship and any possibility of becoming citizens.

This group of people were Americans, if in practice but not in name. They started families. Because there were so few Indian women, intermarriages were common. Punjabi men married Mexican women, creating a hybrid Punjabi Mexican culture in parts of California that still exists today. Yuba County, California was a hotbed of Punjabi Mexican culture and today still has one of the largest Punjabi Sikh populations in the world outside of India. Restaurants in Yuba County are one the few places that serve hybrid Mexican and Indian cuisines.

These families had children, and as these children came of age, they brought their American identities into their Indian heritage. More importantly, they became, whether they liked it or not, the harbingers of Indian culture to mainstream American society. White parents met Indian parents when their children shared schools. White children played with brown children in parks and enjoyed the same rites and rituals of a standard all-American childhood.

Assimilation is the process by which immigrants shed the hallmarks of their home country—such as their language, religion, style of dress, cuisine, and traditions—and replace them with the hallmarks of their adopted country. Assimilation in the United States was popularized as a solution to control the threat of immigrants changing American culture by the sociologist Henry Pratt Fairchild. The goal of assimilation is that after a period of time, usually a generation or two, the descendant of an immigrant is no longer distinguishable from a "mainstream" American.

Throughout American history, there are examples of forced and unforced assimilation. Indigenous children in the United States were forced to attend government-run schools that stamped out any native language or customs they learned at home. Ralph Lifshitz, the son of Ashkenazi Jewish immigrants in the Bronx, New York, changed his last name to Lauren to sound more American when he launched his eponymously named American luxury brand Ralph Lauren.

There is competing literature today by American sociologists on the merits of assimilation. After World War II, when the country started to become more sensitive to issues around race (and we'll see what this looked like in a later chapter), multiculturalism arose as an alternative to assimilation. Unlike assimilation, which assumes that one must lose a part of one's identity to assume a new identity, multiculturalism allows a person to retain multiple racial, ethnic, or national identities. In a multicultural world, an immigrant will never lose all the hallmarks of their homeland, but these hallmarks will be accepted and, even at times, adopted by their new country.

Multiculturalists, particularly American multiculturalists (there is a movement in Europe that is distinct), believe that acceptance of diversity, or of "otherness" between different groups of people, comes from proximity. The closer people are to each other, the more likely they are to accept each other's differences.

There was a stark change in the attitudes of American society toward "Hindus" during World War II, and the early signs of this change can start to be seen in the years leading up to the war. Newspapers regularly advertised the lectures of Mozumdar. Bhagat Singh Thind became a spiritual lecturer and his lectures were advertised in newspapers as well.

One newspaper article, published in 1941 by the *San Francisco Chronicle*, reflects the early changes in attitudes toward Indian Americans in an article about Ram Bagai, the youngest of Bagai's children.

Ram immigrated to the United States when he was one year old and lived with his parents in San Francisco and was raised part time with a German American family brought on by Kala to help with childcare. In 1941, Ram was twenty-six years old and a graduate from the University of Southern California and Stanford University (like his stepfather).

After Stanford, Ram moved to Hollywood where he worked in the film industry. He worked for the German American director William (born Wilhelm) Dieterle. Dieterle directed popular films of the late 1930s such as *The Story of Louis Pasteur*, *The Hunchback of Notre Dame*, and *The Life of Emile Zola*, which won an Academy Award for Best Picture. Ram also worked with the American director Garson Kanin who directed early romantic comedies such as *Tom, Dick, and Harry*, starring Ginger Rogers. He brushed shoulders with the celebrities of the day (he and Katharine Hepburn were the only two witnesses to the wedding of Laurence Olivier). Ram never left Hollywood. He would become the president of the Hollywood Foreign Press Association (the industry group best known today for producing the Golden Globe Awards).

Before becoming a major player in Hollywood, Ram turned his attention to bringing Indian cinema to America. In 1941, he returned from a trip to India bringing four Bollywood films (in the 1940s, India's behemoth film industry was a couple of decades old and already churning out more films a year than Hollywood) to be played in theaters for American audiences. On his arrival back to the United States, the writer John Hobart wrote for the *Chronicle* a very favorable article titled "Through India with Camera and Mascara."

"You may not know this," Hobart writes, "but they make movies in India. . . . In this country you never see an Indian movie; you see French movies and Swedish ones and Chinese ones, but never an Indian one. This state of affairs is going to be rectified in the near future by Mr. Ram M. Bagai." Ram is quoted to have said that he wished the films he brought back would help educate Americans about misconceptions about India.

What's most interesting about Hobart's article is not related to the movie business at all but instead a description of Ram himself. Hobart chose his words decisively.

"Now Mr. Bagai is not a mystical gentleman in a turban"—Hobart writes and in doing so immediately dispels the negative stereotype of "Hindus" in the United States—"but an alert, business-like bronze-skinned young man, aged 26, who wears navy-blue suits and sprinkles his conversation with words like 'cheez' and 'swell.'"

Whether or not he intended to, Ram offered the general, white American public a truer view into what it looked like to be Indian. In making the unknown to be known, articles like the one in the *San Francisco Chronicle* did a lot to open the eyes of the American public to the immigrants and denaturalized citizens of modern-day India and South Asia.

Newspaper articles and editorials that pushed a narrative of "Hindus" contaminating the purity of white America, posing as a menace to American standards of living, and stealing acres of land from more-deserving Americans were slowly gaining less traction and replaced with articles about food, cinema, and culture from India. Public interest in Indian culture was mounting, although one can argue that it never did quite go away. But more importantly, alongside this cultural shift toward a new attitude of the "Hindus" in America came a political shift.

The history of civil rights in the United States has shown us that changes in laws around citizenship, voting, and equality as they pertain to the different groups of people who call the United States home require years to build the public support necessary to create the force for legislative change. Public support for immigrant communities often leads to more accepting interpretations of events or actions taken by that community.

Take for example the legal actions the state of California took to repossess lands owned by Indian Americans after they lost their citizenship. The prevailing narrative among the California newspapers in 1924 was that scarcity in land necessitated such actions. Senator William Langer from North Dakota, years later in 1941, offered a different view. He wrote, "The record made by people from India who have come to this country has been outstanding in art, in medicine, in science, in literature, and in agriculture. . . . Hundreds of thousands of acres of poor alkaline land, considered useless by the people of California, through the hard work of the people from India, were made to produce magnificent fields of wild rice, and the lands became tremendously valuable. Practically all of these were lost to the Indians as a result of the decision of the Supreme Court in 1924—a decision which made no provision for the equalities of these poor people; a decision which is a shameful page in the history of the Supreme Court of the United States."

Senator Langer's statement was one of the earliest shows of support and repudiation of the Sutherland decision in 1924 by any member of the federal government. On December 15, 1943, Senator Langer introduced a bill to return citizenship to the Indian Americans who were denaturalized in 1924. The bill was considered by the Senate Committee on Immigration but did not make it to a vote. The bill, however, did lay the groundwork for the eventual legislation that would restore the right to citizenship to Indian Americans and ultimately strike from the law the white clause for citizenship.

Washington, DC, 2018

I was back in the Library Congress for another book research trip. By now, my trips to the library were like clockwork, I knew the protocols and locations of all my materials like the back of my hand. Visits had become routine and a little predictable. Still, there were moments when I was struck by something about the library itself I hadn't noticed before.

The Library of Congress's Main Reading Room is a circular room that feels more like a coliseum than a library. At the center of the room is the librarian. Surrounding the librarian are circular rows of dimly lit research desks that cast a soft glow against a thick, deep blue carpet. Against the golden, marbled walls are a series of arched passageways and doorways that lead to alcoves of bookshelves and rooms with even more books. In this room, you are always surrounded by books. It makes you feel like you are in the presence of all the world's knowledge. It is astounding.

On this trip, I gathered my materials from the waiting librarian and found a desk toward the back. There was a pack of letters among the Sutherland papers, labeled miscellaneous, that I had to read in case they contained any reference to Thind. The letters were droll, the writing was nearly faded after almost one hundred years of lying in boxes untouched, and my eyes kept wandering to the other people in the room.

And that is when I noticed a group of people—it looked like they were not researchers but on some type of tour—looking up. I followed their gazes and saw it, too. The Main Reading Room is several stories tall. Its walls stretch skyward and end in a domed ceiling replete with beautiful stained glass windows. This wasn't new to me. But what was new was that at the point where the walls domed inward was actually a gallery. I had never noticed this before. And on the gallery were a series of statues. Here was something for me to procrastinate from reading Sutherland's papers. The statues were of people one would expect in a library. There was William Shakespeare, the British playwright, Homer, the ancient Greek storyteller, and Herodotus, the ancient Greek who is credited in the Western world for writing some of the earliest known histories. Among this group was also Sir Isaac Newton, who was neither a writer nor a historian but has more to do with the study of history than the average person might think.

Newton is perhaps best known for his book the *Principia*, which established the mathematics of physics' three laws of motion (published in 1648, the first American edition can be found in the Library of Congress's rare book collection). And it is Newton's third law—every action taken by an object has an equal and opposite reaction—that has consequences not only on the study of physics but also the study of history.

The journey to repealing the white citizenship requirement set by the Naturalization Act of 1790 took over thirty years from the day *United States v. Thind* denaturalized Thind and Indian Americans. I was at the Library of Congress on this particular trip, reading all the miscellany from Sutherland's papers to discover all the events or traces of information that could help explain what ultimately caused the United States to have a change of mind and repeal the white citizenship requirement.

An untold series of events ultimately led to this appeal, and in the final section of this book, I have done my best to describe each of the events that led to the white citizenship requirement's appeal. But the search for cause and effects in history, as it is in physics, isn't always straightforward. Cause and effect can be defined, only to be challenged when new pieces of information are introduced to the system.

I was learning that although the history textbooks I grew up reading were quick to resolutely declare that one event led to another event which led to another event, there was a fine line between the absolute truth of what happened and the story of what occurred. In researching this section of South Asian American history, I've done my best to stay on this line.

Based on all the current historiography of South Asians in the United States, there are two forces that contributed most directly to the repeal of denaturalization for Indians and the abolishment of the white citizenship clause. The first was the rise of civic organizations, born out of Indian communities along the West and East Coasts, that were single-mindedly focused on restoring citizenship. The second force was World War II, which forced the United States to reckon with its history and abetting of race-based discrimination and to consider the role Indians played in securing a victory for the Allies.

Luckily for my research purposes, there was not a lack of books about World War II, one of the most studied eras of human history.

13

War

The travel time between New York City and Washington, DC is long, and I soon realized that swapping my drive for a train ride allowed me to spend a couple of hours collecting my thoughts and organizing my research into a story. Of course, a lot of this time was actually spent scrolling on my phone. There is a meme that turns up on my social media feeds a fair number of times. It's a cartoon with two people. The first person is trying to publish a book on an esoteric, seemingly small piece of history (think South Asian civil rights in the United States, for example). This person has trouble finding a publisher. The publisher is worried that the book, one of the few of its kind, will not have a large enough audience. The second person is trying to publish a book on World War II history. Her book is one of thousands, if not hundreds of thousands, of books about the same subject. And yet, her book is the talk of publishers, who line up to get their chance at buying the manuscript.

World War II is one of the more horrifying moments of human history, with its depth of human tragedy and breadth of geographic impact. If there was a force strong enough to have changed the proverbial axis of humanity, it was World War II. The war weakened European hegemonies, boosted Asian nationalism, accelerated America's rise as a superpower, and gave birth to a global identity entrusted to the United Nations. The war made profound challenges to ideologies like racism, nationalism, and anti-Semitism, which held together the status quo for millions of people. Before they were upended by World War II, these systems of prejudice and discrimination existed in multiple forms around the world: the genocide of the Jewish people and other minority groups in Europe, the subjugation and colonization of peoples across Asia, Africa, and Latin America, and the racist segregation of nonwhite peoples in the United States.

World War II challenged all of these deeply rooted systems of oppression but also laid the foundation for new sets of freedoms. The war helped shape women's rights. With men fighting in the war, women had to fill the roles of men in their local economies, contributing to the normalization of women in the workplace. Economic necessity gave way to cultural changes that challenged sexist status quos. Women's fashion became less restrictive, women thinkers published seminal books on feminism, and home and domestic responsibilities slowly began to be shared across the sexes. (And it wasn't just the course of women's rights, social justice, and human history affected by World War II. Instant ramen, a favorite of people around the world, foodies, and college students alike, was invented by the Japanese to combat food shortages caused by the war.)

The citizenship of South Asian Americans was tremendously impacted by World War II. To understand how and why this happened, we must first take our story out of the United States and journey into the history of a country we've heard a lot about but haven't visited: India.

In March 1939, Mohandas Gandhi began a fast to object to British rule in India, his nonviolent alternative to protesting British colonial rule. India's political consciousness had awakened. Its goal was a united India free from colonialism at the hands of a distant and autocratic empire. Indians desired to be free to govern themselves democratically. But that same year, the British Empire's grasp on India became tighter, as world events made the colonizer more dependent on its prized colony.

Several months later, in September, Germany invaded Poland. In response, Great Britain, alongside France, declared war on Germany. This began World War II. Allied with Great Britain and France was the Soviet Union, and after Japan's bombing of Pearl Harbor, the United States joined and became the Allies. Germany was allied with Italy and Japan; they were called the Axis. The fighting stretched across Europe, Africa, and Asia, engulfing the entire world in total war. Over the course of six years, thirty countries sent over 100 million men and women to battle. Two and a half million of those soldiers were men from India.

The British Indian Army was a military force under the command of the British Empire. Its purpose was to maintain British control and authority in South Asia. Before they became allies in World War II, the British were particularly concerned about the threat of a Soviet-led invasion of India via Afghanistan. At the onset of World War II, the British government did not anticipate the need to mobilize the British Indian Army, with the exception of deploying a small number of infantrymen to Europe to help defend against Germany's advancement through Western Europe (France would fall to the Germans in 1940).

India's involvement in World War II was controversial. As a part of the British Empire, the deployment of Indian troops to the war effort was a command that local Indian governments and people had little say in. Serving in the army was a lucrative enough career that the British never had to conscript soldiers and could rely entirely on paid volunteers. (By the end of the war, the British Indian Army was the largest volunteer force in history.) By 1939, however, deep-rooted resentments against colonialism had taken hold of India's national government, led by Indians. Over the last half century, Indians had taken to military action, hunger strikes, political lobbying, and global mobilization (the Ghadar Party in the United States, for example) with the cause of winning independence from the British. The desire for self-rule was so strong that the Indian government attempted to make fighting in the war conditional on India receiving independence.

London did not agree to this proposition. That did not stop local Indian politicians from organizing the Quit India movement to protest the war. This resulted in Great Britain imprisoning tens of thousands of politicians for dissent. One Indian leader named Subhash Chandra Bose even attempted to recruit the favor of Adolf Hitler to provide military capabilities to the Indian independence effort. Bose also helped the Japanese Empire recruit Indian soldiers for an army to fight alongside the Axis and against the Allies, specifically the British.

Two years into the onset of the war, India's geographic position made it a vital strategic player in the Allies' effort against Japan. Japan's aspirations was to be the sole power in the Asian continent, to invade and conquer lands occupied by the Soviet Union, China, and the British Empire, and to be the dominant naval and aerial power in the waters of the Pacific Ocean. As the war raged in the west, Japan looked eastward and on December 7, 1941 bombed Pearl Harbor, attacking the United States without any formal declaration of war preceding the bombing. (The bombing was not actually supposed to be a surprise. Japan originally intended for the bombing to occur half an hour after the formal delivery of a declaration of war. However, the declaration, which was transmitted over encrypted Morse code to Japan's embassy in Washington, DC could not be decrypted in time.)

The attack on Pearl Harbor forced the United States to enter a war that had mixed public support. On the one hand, there was the need to defend America against attack. On the other hand, America's doctrine of isolationism, first advocated by President George Washington, warned against the new country from becoming entangled and embroiled in conflicts thousands of miles from its own borders. Still reeling from World War I, which was supposed to be the war to end all wars, isolationists considered the events in Europe to be too removed from North America to warrant the efforts of the United States. However, the United States had aspirations for dominance of the Pacific, so the attack on Pearl Harbor could not go unavenged. President Franklin D. Roosevelt signed the declaration of war against Japan the very next day, joining the Allies. Great Britain declared war on Japan, too, technically announcing their declaration nine hours before the United States.

Great Britain's declaration of war against Japan made India a prime target for Japan's next attack. Japan's strategy was to invade the European colonies through Southeast Asia, reasoning that the colonial governments were preoccupied by war efforts on their home turfs. After invading Dutch possessions in the southeast, Japan moved northward to the British colony of Burma. To conquer Burma would provide the positioning necessary for a Japanese attack and invasion of India. Preventing this was a primary concern for the British Indian Army.

Whereas the British feared a Japanese invasion of India, the Japanese were more interested in the decolonization of India. Indian self-rule, the Japanese reasoned, with the Japanese support of Indian independence would create a vital ally for the Japanese Empire in the region.

The Japanese fought Great Britain elsewhere in Asia not just with guns and tanks but also with deft propaganda that picked at the already festering wounds of Britain's Indian soldiers. It was wrong, the Japanese contended, for Indians to risk their lives for a government that was thousands of miles away, on the other side of the world. It was wrong to fight for an empire that for hundreds of years wielded total economic and political power over India. It was wrong to fight for the security of a colonizer that did not care for the freedom of the soldiers in its largest force. One piece of Japanese propaganda in particular stands out. The propaganda consisted of a cartoon watercolor. At the center stood an Indian man, standing tall and proud, his arms crossed over his chest as he stared off the advancements of short, fat, and angry-looking cartoon men representing Great Britain, China, and the United States.

To continue its fight for the hearts and minds of the British Indian Army, Japan even turned its attention to the treatment of Indians in the United States. The United States could not even dignify India with equal treatment of Indians within its borders. The

United States could not, and would not, even give citizenship to Indians, making the stark implication that the United States thought Indians were inferior. And not only did the United States think Indians were not worthy of American citizenship; the United States had also given citizenship to Indians only to strip it away in an unceremonious disregard for their rights. It was hypocritical, the Japanese propaganda contended, for the United States to expect Indians to join and fight for the Allies.

Japan's efforts to turn Indian sentiment away from the British were not successful. Throughout World War II, as politicians in India strategized for independence, British Indian soldiers fought in North Africa, East Africa, Iraq, Persia, Syria, Lebanon, Hong Kong, Malaya, Singapore, Borneo, Burma, France, Italy, and Greece. Although India's desire for independence was strong, it also had cultural and historical ties to Great Britain that precluded it from entering any alliance with a declared enemy of the United Kingdom. Even after India successfully won its freedom in 1947, the country decided to join the Commonwealth of Nations, an informal political organization of independent countries that were previously British colonies but still chose to view Great Britain's monarchy as a symbolic figurehead.

In the United States, however, Japan's propaganda on America's treatment of Indian Americans did strike a chord among politicians who were forced to confront the hypocrisy of America's pursuit of freedom abroad while denying it to so many at home.

January 6, 1941, Washington, DC

Almost one year before the attack on Pearl Harbor, President Roosevelt was priming the country for the possibility of war. In his State of the Union speech, Roosevelt laid out four principle freedoms that guaranteed the "rights of men of every creed and every race, wherever they might live." These principles were the freedom of speech, freedom of worship, freedom from want, and freedom from fear. Roosevelt's remarks have been dubbed by historians the Four Freedoms Speech, and it did less to win support for the

United States' entry to World War II than elevate American dialogue around the need to preserve and uphold basic human freedoms afforded to every person regardless of their race, color, or nationality. The call to fight for what was morally good was uniquely American, Roosevelt contended. The Four Freedoms Speech represents a remarkable shift that dominated much of American history in the second half of the twentieth century. The United States had a moral obligation to uphold its ideals not just within its own borders but around the world.

Roosevelt made the distinctions between good and evil very clear. On the side of the good was democracy and its promise to equally preserve the rights afforded to everyone around the world. On the side of the bad was fascism and its threat to the freedoms of individuals at the hands of the power hungry. But these distinctions, meant to demonstrate and define the United States' positioning on the global stage (and to draw lines between potential allies and foes, the rhetoric of Roosevelt's speech laid the groundwork for later presidents' use of "you're either with us, or you're with them" tactics in foreign policy), instead highlighted the hypocrisy of the treatment of people of different, nonwhite races in the United States by the American government.

Organizations like the National Association for the Advancement of Colored People (NAACP) hit their stride in continually lobbying Congress, initiating legal proceedings in the courts, and galvanizing public opinion to desegregate the U.S. military, which did not let Black and white soldiers serve alongside each other on and off the battlefield. (It wouldn't be until the Korean War that segregation in the military officially ended, not just by policy but by practice, too.) The movement for desegregation transcended the military and spread to all facets of American life. It was during World War II that organizations like the Congress of Racial Equality (CORE) organized some of the first sit-ins in Chicago restaurants, the first picket lines in Saint Louis, and the first Freedom Rides (in which Black activists and ordinary citizens purposely rode in buses across state lines and into segregated cities) across the American South. The United States had to first practice freedom and equality for all people at home before spreading the word abroad. Although a much smaller minority group, Indian Americans took this to heart and seized the moment to start organizing.

Indian American political organization really began in the 1930s. Prior to the decade, Indian immigrants were trying to do what most immigrants do when they first arrive in the United States—they were trying to make a new life. The priority was to secure jobs and make money that could be sent home or used to build a life in America. Once work was found, or in other cases education completed, attention shifted to starting and building families. Families became the units around which civic organizations formed. These organizations started off as largely social but began to take on more political leanings after the denaturalization of 1924. In the immediate aftermath of the Sutherland decision, political action was still largely at the individual level. The largest known action was that of S. G. Pandit, Thind's lawyer, who took his own denaturalization case to court in 1926 to demonstrate its unfairness. Curiously, Pandit won his case on a legal principle called res judicata, which held that the outcome of a case could not be changed once decided and upheld by a court. He is the only known Indian American to have his citizenship restored during the period of denaturalization, and due to his case, the United States did slow down its efforts in denaturalization.

Starting in the 1930s, Indian American civic organizations arguably became more political as they received support and financial backing from the Indian government. A review of primary source documents reveals direct correspondences between pro-Independence Indian government officials and American organization leaders such as the India Welfare League and the India League of America. There is little to no evidence of this type of communication happening in the earlier decades of Indian American history.

Studying history is almost like reviewing a photo negative of what actually happened. People tend to record what happened and not necessarily what didn't happen. And sometimes the events that didn't happen become more interesting than the events that did happen. (The wild popularity, at least around history nerd circles, of alternate history fiction speaks to this.)

Take, for example, the domestic forces within the United States that ultimately led to repeal of the naturalization ban on people from South Asia. It wasn't Indian American organizations on the West Coast that wrote the majority of known letters to congressmen, public intellectuals, business leaders, and prominent American politicians. The letter campaigns and lobbying were almost all initiated by the India Welfare League and India League of America, organizations that were based on the East Coast. The East Coast had a much smaller Indian population than the West Coast but demonstrated to be political in a way that the West Coast was not. To understand this, we need to delve into the experiences of a senator from North Dakota.

Arizona, 1943

North Dakota senator William Langer had been to Arizona only once in his childhood. When the senator received an invitation from the Democratic Women of Maricopa County to present a talk, he took the chance for another visit. Langer's talk was open to the public, and over 500 people attended to meet the senator from North Dakota. The attendees were Democrats and Republicans, but to Langer's surprise, almost 200 of them were Indian. They did not know Langer personally, nor did they know of his politics. They weren't even members of the Democratic Women of Maricopa County. They had come to ask Senator Langer for citizenship.

Langer was struck by how ordinarily American the Indians seemed. "They were very fine citizens," he later told Senate colleagues on the immigration committee. "None of them had any trouble at any time." The Indians lived outside of Phoenix and in the surrounding areas, in largely agricultural communities. "They were small farmers," Langer described. "Some of them had truck gardens, some of them had quarter sections of land where they were raising lettuce."

The Indians Langer met were pretty blunt in their request. "They asked me why they could not be admitted for citizenship." Langer wasn't even aware that Indian immigrants couldn't become citizens. He wasn't even aware there was an Indian American community in the United States prior to his visit to Maricopa. He pledged to look into the issue.

One man among the crowd of Indians introduced himself to Langer. Mubarek Ali Khan was the president of the India Welfare League of America, headquartered in New York City. One cannot suspect Khan was behind the hundreds of Indians at Langer's talk.

Khan was a young man, in his early twenties, when he took a job as a sailor on a ship bound for the United States. When the ship arrived at port in New York City, sometime between 1920 and 1922 (primary sources provide conflicting dates), Khan literally jumped ship and never returned aboard. He started a new life in the United States. He was part of a community of men, primarily Indian and mostly Hindu and Muslim, who were former sailors that settled along the United States' East Coast, mainly in New York City.

Khan understood the need to humanize and show how ordinary and nonthreatening Indians were in the United States. He showed Langer photographs from his son's wedding, his daughter at her primary school with her friends, and later photographs of his daughter at her high school in Arizona. These were all "typical scenes" of American life, Langer noted.

Instead of returning home to North Dakota, Langer asked Khan to show him the rest of the Indian American community. Together, they drove north to California, where they passed by the rice fields Indian farmers had cultivated. Langer met with California governor Earl Warren who attested that Indians hadn't deprived Americans of scarce land but instead cultivated land that was previously thought to be arid. (Ultimately it was Indians' comfort with temperatures above 100°F and knowledge of working land in extreme heat that provided them with a farming acumen other Californians lacked.)

"It just seemed to me," Langer remarked, "a matter of simple justice to give these people a chance to become citizens."

It was Khan's idea for Langer to travel to New York City. Langer shared the following account to his Senate colleagues.

"There are a few [Indians] in New Jersey and a few in New York City. In New York, I was amazed; some of them are graduates of Harvard. In New York City they are doctors. I met a man named J.J. Singh who graduated from Harvard. . . . They are all in the trades and sciences. . . . I met a leading dentist in New York City who is one of them."

"It just seemed pitiful to me that these people should not have a chance to become citizens, because they seemed to want it very, very, badly in discussing it with them," he concluded.

Langer's meeting with J. J. Singh was no accident. In a profile of the Indian man who would become credited with garnering support within the U.S. Congress to grant citizenship to Indians, the *New Yorker* called Singh a "lone-wolf lobbyist." *New Yorker* magazine quoted a congressman who was swayed by Singh's lobbying as saying, "He's got something the others lack. Maybe it's because his heart's in it." From the back of his office in Midtown Manhattan, Singh devised his political strategy. Singh's strong ties with Congress helped him assemble three key lawmakers who would bring legislation to the Congress floor. First, there was William Langer who would take care of the Senate. Next were Emanuel Celler, a representative from New York, and Clare Boothe Luce, a representative from Connecticut.

Singh had his team. Langer was already in his corner. Now it was just time to persuade Celler and Luce.

14

Resolution

New York City, 1943

By the early twentieth century, the United States was transforming from a country characterized by agriculture to a global superpower on the forefront of commerce and manufacturing centered on its largest cities. Although cities like San Francisco and Chicago wielded considerable influence in their regions in the West and Midwest, respectively, no city could compare to New York City. The tallest buildings in the United States, and the world—the Empire State Building, the Chrysler Building, and Rockefeller Center—were all already iconic symbols of American industrial and commercial power. If the future of the global economy lay in the emergence of the United States, then New York City's influence would reach far beyond the Atlantic Ocean.

New York City was the center of the American economy. Most companies were headquartered in Manhattan, and if they were not headquartered, they at least had an office in one of the hundreds of skyscrapers. Outside of Washington, DC, foreign nations maintained consulates on the tiny island bordered by the East and Hudson Rivers. The United Nations would choose New York City for its global headquarters, eschewing old world cities like London or Paris that might have held this honor in a previous time.

Immigration cemented New York City's status as a global hub. In the United States, New York City remained the largest entry point for immigrants seeking a new life in America. Of course, immigrants from Asia were less likely to arrive from the Atlantic Ocean than the Pacific Ocean, so the number of South Asian immigrants, specifically, that arrived in New York's Ellis Island was less than the number that arrived to San Francisco's Angel Island. (The stories of these East Coast immigrants from South Asia have been chronicled in books such as *Bengali Harlem* by Vivek Bald.)

Echoing the story of Mubarek Ali Khan, most of these immigrants were men who traveled the world as sailors. Although the South Asian population on the West Coast was largely Sikh and Hindu, many of the immigrants on the East Coast were Muslim, reflecting the religious diversity that was prevalent in colonial India. These sailors settled in New York, and because there were so few female immigrants, they married and settled into Black and Latinx communities like their counterparts on the West Coast.

New York City served as the first stop for trade into the United States, and so it attracted merchants from around the world importing food and goods. One of these men was J. J. Singh who sold Indian fabrics and saris to Manhattan's elite out of a store on East 56th Street called India Arts and Crafts.

In his apartment on East 44th Street on Manhattan's then Upper East Side, J. J. Singh looked through the window and out to the East River. As a businessman and as an Indian, Singh wanted two things. First, he desired Indian independence. Second, he wanted Indians to have the right to become American citizens. Singh's second wish was crucial if there was to be a healthy trade partnership between the United States and India. India could not do business with the United States if the United States didn't consider Indians to be equal to Americans.

J. J. Singh was born Jagjit Singh in Rawalpindi, a city that was in the northwestern corner of British India and today is in modern-day Pakistan. After coming to the United States in 1926 to set up an import business, J. J. Singh decided to stay. He enjoyed the culture, the parties, and most importantly, the tailored suits. Singh was born Sikh, but in his adulthood, he shaved his beard and cut his hair. His large, bushy eyebrows crawled like caterpillars across his face as he talked.

There was something about Singh that made him magnetic. The *New Yorker* ran a flattering profile of Singh titled "One-Man Lobby," a nod to his ability to endear himself to those in power. "J.J always gives the audience the impression that he's either just arrived from somewhere or is just about to take off for somewhere—somewhere important," one of his friends told the *New Yorker*. It was Singh's idea to take his charm to Washington and try to get Congress to override the Supreme Court's decision in *United States v. Thind* with a new piece of legislation.

For an idea to become law in the United States, it must undergo a deceptively simple process. First, a member of Congress must agree to sponsor the idea and write a bill that explains the purpose and the terms of the law. The bill can then be introduced to Congress either through the House or the Senate, depending on if the sponsor is a representative or senator. Once it is introduced, the bill is then reviewed by the relevant committee in the House or Senate. The committee debates the merits of the bill, makes necessary changes, and votes on whether to advance the bill. If the committee votes yes, the bill is then presented to the entire chamber for a debate and larger vote. (This is also when members of Congress can walk across the street to the Library of Congress and use a section of the library that is only open to elected officials and their staff for further research.) If the bill passes in one chamber of Congress, it is then sent to the remaining chamber to undergo a similar process. If both chambers of Congress vote yes on a bill, it is then taken to the president of the United States. If the president signs the bill, the bill becomes law. If the president does not sign the bill, it is vetoed and sent back to Congress.

In order to undergo this process for Indian American citizenship, J. J. Singh needed to assemble a team of allies across Congress who could carry his idea through the congressional system and make it to law.

The first member Singh recruited was Senator William Langer, or "Wild Bill," of North Dakota. The senator had traveled across the American Southwest and West, meeting Indians who were practically Americans in everything but name. He brought back his findings to Washington, DC, showing photos of the people he had met. They were not a threat or menace. They were ordinary Americans.

Singh had two members of the House of Representatives he wanted to recruit to complete his trifecta with Senator Langer. Connecticut congresswoman Clare Boothe Luce and New York congressman Emanuel Celler. Both had been selected as they had personal relationships with Singh and had demonstrated sympathy publicly to immigrants from countries outside of Europe. (Congresswoman Luce had publicly denounced the United States' Chinese Exclusionary Acts, comparing them to the work of Hitler and the Nazi Party.)

Clare Boothe Luce was the twenty-ninth woman to serve in the U.S. House of Representatives and the first from Connecticut. Luce was elected to Congress after campaigning to end World War II and focus on national security and employment. (That she campaigned is significant; many earlier women in Congress took their seats due to "widow's succession," a rule that allowed a woman to serve in her husband's place if he died before completing his time in office.) Luce's husband was Henry Luce, the publisher who owned *Time*, *Life*, *Fortune*, and *Sports Illustrated*. Henry and Singh were society friends. They attended the same parties, donated to the same charities, and attended the same opening nights on Broadway. But it was Clare Luce who dazzled Singh. Before she was a congresswoman, Luce was a writer. In 1936, she wrote a play called *The Women*, a Broadway production with forty female leads. Her profile appeared on the cover of *Life*. She traveled to Asia in 1941 where she interviewed General Douglas MacArthur. Luce's tour of Asia concluded in India, where she met Jawaharlal Nehru, an activist for Indian independence (he would become India's first prime minister in 1947) and Singh's hero and political mentor. It was rumored Nehru had personally sent Singh to the United States to build goodwill between the two countries. When Luce returned to the United States, she and her husband hosted Singh in their home for the summer. In 1942, Luce ran as a Republican and was elected to the U.S. House of Representatives, representing Connecticut from Fairfield County. With her election, Singh knew he had secured the second ally of his desired triumvirate.

The third and final recruit was also a member of the House of Representatives but the opposite of Congresswoman Luce in almost every way possible. In 1943, Emanuel Celler was serving his twentieth year in Congress. He had been elected the same year that Justice George Sutherland wrote his decision in *United States v. Thind*. Celler was born and bred in Brooklyn and was the son of German immigrants of both Jewish and Catholic descent. He represented his hometown borough (and later Queens through several rounds of redistricting) in Washington, DC. Like a true son of Brooklyn, Celler would also die in Brooklyn but not before serving the fifth-longest congressional career in the United States and the longest congressional career in New York State history. He was a Democrat and a graduate of Columbia University, where he earned his law degree. Celler was an experienced legislator and had the legislative acumen J. J. Singh needed to get congressional votes. More importantly, Celler was experienced in legislating immigration law. He opposed the Johnson-Reed Immigration Act of 1924 when it was introduced. The act sought to instill a quota system to decrease the number of immigrants from southern and eastern Europe and to prevent whiteness in America from becoming, well, no longer white. The act disproportionally affected Catholic and Jewish immigrants from coming to the United States. Celler saw this as directly antithetical to American values (as well as a direct threat to the American economy, which relied so heavily on immigrants). Eliminating immigration quotas and creating a free and open immigration system became Celler's main legislative goals.

Singh's relationship with Congresswoman Luce was a strong friendship buoyed by a love for New York City society. In Congressman Celler, Singh found a mentor, and in Singh, Congressman Celler found an eager student. Of Singh, Congressman Celler has said, "He was sagacious and delicate. He never made a nuisance of himself. He didn't have to wine 'em and dine 'em, because he had a good cause and he had the facts in his hand. The stenographers said he had oomph. They were fascinated by him. He had a rarity, like a prince with a jewel on his forehead."

With the support of Senator Langer, Congresswoman Luce, and Congressman Celler, Singh had assembled his triumvirate. Langer would introduce the bill on the Senate floor. Luce and Celler would cosponsor the bill in the House. All they had to do now was propose a solution and draft the bill.

The team of four couldn't be too extreme. Taking into account their political leanings and party affiliations, they averaged out to a centrist group and agreed their bill needed to accomplish their goals without giving anybody who opposed the idea of the United States being a country for more than just white people room to argue that the bill would pose a threat to mainstream American whiteness. The first part of the bill allowed for "Indians from Asia"—modern-day Indians, Pakistanis, and Bangladeshis—to become United States citizens. The second part of the bill, opposed by Celler but necessary for compromise, placed a yearly quota of one hundred immigrants on Indians in Asia who could enter the country.

The wording of the bill was simple. And in 1944, what became known as the Luce-Celler Act was introduced to Congress.

Washington, DC, 1945

On April 26, 1945, the seventy-ninth Congress convened for its first session on a hearing before the committee on immigration to debate "a bill to permit all people from India residing in the United States to be naturalized." Attending the hearing were thirteen senators from Florida, Maryland, South Carolina, Mississippi, Arkansas, North Carolina, California, Ohio, Minnesota, Delaware, Michigan, Missouri, and North Dakota. Georgia senator Richard B. Russell presided as chairman.

The debate opened with a statement from Edward J. Shaughnessy, a special assistant to the commissioner of the Immigration and Nationalization Service. Shaughnessy started by giving a very short history of Mozumdar's and Thind's legal cases.

"For ordinary purposes the East Indian was neither white nor African black because as of that time only those two races were racially eligible for naturalization. They recognized that from a scientific and ethnological standpoint, and other purposes, the question was debatable. In the meantime, prior to that, a few courts had differed on the question and had naturalized a few East Indian.... That explains the reason why there is a necessity for a bill of this nature if some relief is to be given to the East Indians presently in the United States."

Shaughnessy approved the bill.

Next, the committee called Dr. John M. Cooper, a professor of anthropology at Catholic University in Washington, DC. Senator Eastland of Mississippi started by giving his own views on citizenship: "I think, and I am just speaking frankly, that citizenship in this country should go to people who intermarry, assimilate, become part of the white race." Eastland then asked Dr. Cooper a rather blunt question: "Could the Indians of this country be assimilated?"

Dr. Cooper answered yes.

Finally, South Carolina Senator Maybank produced a letter addressed to the committee and submitted it to the hearing's official record. The letter began, "I regard this legislation as important and desirable, and I believe that its enactment will help us to win the war and to establish a secure peace. I am sure that your committee is aware of the great services that India has rendered to the United Nations in their war against the Axis. The Indian Army, raised entirely by voluntary enlistment, has fought with great skill and courage." The letter went on to talk about Indians closer to home.

"The present statutory provisions that discriminate against persons of East Indian descent provoke ill-feeling, now serve no useful purpose, and are incongruous and inconsistent with the dignity of both of our peoples."

"It is my hope that the Congress will take steps to remove the present provisions of our immigration and naturalization laws that discriminate against persons of East Indian descent."

The writer ended with his signature—Franklin D. Roosevelt.

It was time for the Senate and the House to vote.

In July 1946, J. J. Singh was invited to the White House along with nine other Indian men. He was asked to stand behind President Harry Truman, who sat at his desk wearing a bow tie and signed the Luce-Celler Act into law. Indians could become American citizens.

In a photograph taken by the White House photographer, Singh is seen smiling down on President Truman. The president gifted Singh with the pen he used to sign the law. Singh was photographed with the pen and a wide smile. The president's gift signaled to the American press and the public at the time that it was J. J Singh who was entirely responsible for fighting for Indians' right to citizenship. Singh was a freedom fighter, not just in India but also in the United States. What the press or public did not know was that Singh was just the final step of what had been a very long journey for scores of Indian Americans that began in Seattle in 1904.

The Luce-Celler Act won Indian Americans the right to become citizens and be treated equally as Americans in their adopted homeland. The act did not repeal the Naturalization Act of 1790, but it did significantly weaken it. More importantly, the Luce-Celler Act was the final legislative blow on a period of American history that demonstrates that the United States is not, and has never been, a country for only white people.

The Naturalization Act of 1790 would ultimately be replaced by the Immigration Act of 1952, the first of a series of legislation that paved the United States' immigration system into what exists today. Although the system is far from perfect, it does establish that any person, regardless of their skin color or country of origin, has the right to become an American citizen. The act's repeal signifies an America that our founding fathers might not have expected but would have approved of. The United States of

America has always been, and will always be, a great experiment on what can happen when we try to build a nation that brings people together instead of one that divides. And this experiment is proven, not in the halls of Congress or the White House but in the lives of average Americans who each day demonstrate what is possible in this country.

Washington, DC, 2018

On a Thursday night in August, I left the Library of Congress for the last time in my research for this book. My research on the legislative debates that led to Congress's passing of the Luce-Cellar Act was complete. The weather was warm and muggy, and although the sun started to set, there was still enough light to walk down the National Mall. The Library of Congress, the United States Capitol, and the George Washington Memorial are all stark, white buildings. Walking with the Capitol building behind me and the Washington Memorial in front of me, I realized Washington, DC was a fitting place to end this story.

Before any of the buildings on the Mall were erected, before Congress even settled on this land for their capitol, before even the creation of this country that would require a congress, the Nacotchtank people called this land their home. Nacotchtank families and communities lived in villages on Capitol Hill. The Nacotchtank economy thrived on farming the lands that are now the Library of Congress and U.S. Supreme Court. The white marble and gneiss stones used for building construction across the Mall were all mined in quarries around the Potomac River Valley by Black Americans, free and enslaved.

The United States was founded on land that already belonged to people of color. The United States was built by people of color. The United States is what it is today because of people of color.

The United States was never just a country for white people. This country has always required and benefited from people of all colors who believed in a shared dream that all men and women are created equal.

For far too long, people in power used the U.S. government to institutionalize racism to prevent our democracy from truly reflecting the people it served. These people were motivated by fear of losing an America that they believed was white. This white America never actually existed but was a lie used to make some people feel superior and other people less-than in order to maintain the status quo. The status quo became more difficult to maintain as the unstoppable progress of immigration brought the United States into the modern era. Lies had to be created to separate our nation's dependence on immigrants from its mythological white identity. The Naturalization Act of 1790 was one such lie. For 162 years, over half the span of the United States' history, immigrants who were not white could not become American citizens for no good reason.

As a brown American woman and the daughter of immigrants, discovering this stark example of racism institutionalized in the American government was shocking and spurred me to write this book. But the Naturalization Act of 1790 and stories of Mozumdar, Thind, and Kala Bagai led to an even more important discovery: There were people like me in the pages of history of the United States, a country I am so proud to call home despite never quite feeling like I belonged. The truth is, I always belonged.

I continued my walk until I reached the Lincoln Memorial. With President Lincoln to my back, I sat on the steps. This has always been my favorite view of our nation's capital. Looking out and over the reflection pool, the buildings seem smaller and more realistic.

America will never be only a white country. I had all the evidence that night. There were the notebooks and books in my backpack and the hundreds of historical documents on my phone, many older than the steps I was sitting on.

My research was one beat in a cacophonous national discourse that has become impossible to ignore. From Bollywood movies and Korean dramas on Netflix to social media activism like the #StopAsianHate movement, it's exceedingly clear that there is no longer any appetite to accept attempts at whitewashing American politics, culture, or history.

As Americans, we will continue to struggle to reckon and reconcile race and what it means to be an American. I have so many friends whose grandparents immigrated to this country and became citizens. If my own grandparents came to the United States before 1952, the year my own dad was born, my grandparents could not have become citizens. Progress is progressing. My parents immigrated to this country and became citizens. But the legacy of whiteness as a requirement for American citizenship has evolved into a bias that the default, mainstream, or "normal" American is a white person. This bias looms over us all.

It looms over every colored American, or aspiring American, who has chafed at being asked "Where are you from?" but deep down struggling with answering for themselves, "Who am I?"

It looms over every colored child in American schools today who read American history textbooks and do not find people who look like them.

It looms when we talk about how America should be governed, a conversation where there's so much fear from everybody, white people included, that the America being built for the future is an America that does not look like them.

Most dangerously, the legacy of whiteness looms in how we construct American identity. It is no coincidence that the history books I loved growing up, written by white authors, exclude significant portions of nonwhite American history. Perhaps their intentions were benign, but these are the examples of racial biases that are ingrained in all of us and create dangerous stereotypes around who is American and who is not.

If François Barbé-Marbois, our French friend who wondered what made an American an American, ever saw me in person, I doubt he would have thought I was an American. Just based on the color of my skin, he would have assumed (depending on how good his geography was) I was somewhere from the East. It is funny to me that over 200 years later, Marbois's point of view is still quite common. People of color who are citizens of the United States are never simply American. We are Indian American or South Asian American or Chinese American or African American. These are labels that we can sometimes define and assign to ourselves, but sometimes these are identities that are defined and assigned to us by others. That's the funny thing about identity. It is based not just on how we see ourselves but how others see ourselves as well.

This is why the myth of American whiteness is so harmful to Americans of color. The feeling of exclusion becomes a barrier self-imposed by people of color that ends up being stronger than anything a racist law can do. There are no laws prohibiting the telling of South Asian American history. The stories never got told because the people tasked with telling our country's story believed South Asian American history wasn't important or, more sadly, didn't exist. We must all think critically about whether our internalized notions of who is an American are truly reflective of the America we live in today.

The only path forward is to look back and realize that the people of color who made up America from the beginning have had the same issues that we have today, and yet here we are. I am a South Asian American author writing a book about South Asian American history. Mindy Kaling is a South Asian American woman and one of the most powerful women in Hollywood. Anjali Sud, another South Asian American woman, leads Vimeo and is one of the youngest female CEOs in America. A Black South Asian American woman, Kamala Harris, has been elected vice-president of the United States. Multiple levels of American society are reflecting the diversity of America that has always existed.

What threatens America is not differences between its citizens. It's trying to force homogeneity among its citizens. As citizens, either by choice or by birth, we are united by a shared obligation to each other and to our country. And we can fulfill this obligation to its highest vision regardless of the color of our skin. This is because we are all more similar than we are different.

Through the course of my research, I discovered many materials that did not make it into this story. Many of these materials can be accessed by visiting the research libraries I've described. A majority of these materials are all online and available for free at the South Asian American Digital Archive. There is one digital material I want to bring up as I end this book, a diary Rani Bagai kept in 1955. In the diary, Bagai wrote of dinner parties in California and her travels to London. She kept track of stock prices at the end of almost each day. One diary entry, written on Friday, January 7, 1955, stood out to me. Bagai writes that she went to her son Ram's house for dinner. At dinner were several guests including Bhagat Singh Thind and his wife. That Bagai and Thind enjoyed a friendship, or an acquaintanceship, struck me as a happy ending. Akhoy Kumar Mozumdar had passed away two years prior in 1953. His story lived on in the minds and work of his followers. I do not know if he ever met or knew of Bagai or Thind. But knowing that Bagai's and Thind's journeys intersected made me believe in the strength of the South Asian American community.

We don't know what they might have talked about that night at dinner. Bagai writes that the dinner group ate aloo parathas, an Indian bread stuffed with a savory potato filling, and had kheer for dessert. Aloo paratha and kheer are comfort foods I ate as a kid. Had I brought any of these foods into school for lunch, I would have been made fun of. For the longest time, these were foods that I associated with my "brown side." And now, here I was, reading a piece of American history from 1955 Los Angeles where two Americans who looked like me ate the same foods I did. This scene was what I literally was searching for at the onset of my research journey. My childhood self needed to see scenes like this in her American history books. Well, now the next child in Queens or anywhere in the United States with an affection for American history can.

What also struck me from reading Bagai's diary, and even the diaries of other characters in this book like Justice Sutherland, was that we never quite know what small detail or action might spark a connection between two people separated by time and space. This is what I love most about history: you never know what will make you relate to a person from the past, but once you do, that connection is binding. As Americans, we have a shared history. And from our shared history, we can all find common ground and finally see and accept America for what it has always been. This is what makes me feel so hopeful for America.

Today, I live in lower Manhattan, across the street from Federal Hall, the site where President George Washington took his oath of office and where the Naturalization Act of 1790 was signed into law. The steps of Federal Hall are open to the public, and when the sun is shining, New Yorkers of all colors sit on the steps of the stone-gray building. Tourists come to this area to take photos of other nearby landmarks such as Trinity Church and the Stock Exchange. I watch them and notice that almost every time they take a photo of Federal Hall, their photos are full of life: Asian grandmothers with umbrellas to protect themselves from the sun, Black students with backpacks on lunch break from the high school down the street, a Latino man who plays his violin leaning on a column. On these steps of America's first government is a picture of how diverse America has always been, and it is a reminder to me every day of how diverse America will always be. And this is why all Americans of color should always feel like they belong. We are from here, and we are here to stay.

Note on Research

I wrote this book to prove that someone like me can. I hope I was able to show how fun and easy discovering our country's history can be. Asian American history, and in particular South Asian American history, is still a growing area of American history. I've done my best to compose a complete picture of the lives and events that defined the American experience for early South Asian immigrants. But history is additive, and it's my hope that someone reading this will make their own visit to the Library of Congress (you get to keep your official library card forever) or go online to the South Asian American Digital Archive and find a piece of history I undoubtedly overlooked. To make it easier for the next fellow researcher, I've included a list of sources to start with below:

Angel Island Immigration Station Foundation
https://www.aiisf.org/
The Bancroft Library at Berkeley
https://www.lib.berkeley.edu/libraries/bancroft-library
Library of Congress
https://www.loc.gov/
South Asian American Digital Archive
https://www.saada.org/
Online Resources for A. K. Mozumdar
http://mozumdar.org/index.html
Online Resources for Bhagat Singh Thind
https://www.bhagatsinghthind.com/

Acknowledgments

It would be impossible to write any book about South Asian American history without the people who work to preserve our history. I would like to thank the librarians and staff of the following institutions: The Bancroft Library at Berkeley, Library of Congress, South Asian American Digital Archive, and Angel Island Immigration Station Foundation.

I'm indebted to my friends who read early drafts of this book and gave advice and encouragement during difficult moments in writing. Thank you all for helping me believe in my voice.

My journey writing this book would never have started if Sam Freedman of Columbia University hadn't taken a chance on me. And my journey could not have reached its heights without the guidance and support of my editor, Jasper Chang. Thank you both.

About the Author

GEETIKA RUDRA is an amateur history buff with a deep love of American history. She is the daughter of Indian immigrants from Queens. She lives in Manhattan with her book collection.